Seeking Jesus in Contemplation and Discernment

Seeking Jesus in Contemplation and Discernment

by
Robert Faricy, S.J.

With a Preface
by
Father Michael Scanlan, T.O.R.

CHRISTIAN CLASSICS, INC.
WESTMINSTER, MARYLAND
1987

ABOUT THE AUTHOR

Robert Faricy, S.J., is Professor of Spirituality at the Gregorian University in Rome, and is widely respected as a lecturer and author. Among his publications are *The Spirituality of Teilhard de Chardin* and *Praying*.

Published in 1983 by: MICHAEL GLAZIER, INC. 1723 Delaware Avenue, Wilmington, Delaware 19806 and Dominican Publications, St. Saviour's, Dublin, Ireland. Reprinted 1987 by Christian Classics, Inc., P.O. Box 30, Westminster, MD, 21157

Reprinted 1989

Library of Congress Catalog Card Number: 83-81843

ISBN: 0-87061 1429

Printed in Great Britain by Bell & Bain Ltd, Glasgow

. . .

Dedicated
to
Mother M. Angelica

CONTENTS

PREFACE

I am pleased to introduce the perfect match presented by this book: the right author for the right subject.

The subject is right because it meets an important need for instruction. The current emphasis on a personal relationship with Jesus and experiential knowledge of the power of the Holy Spirit has created a demand for clear instruction on the relationship between these experiences and traditional Catholic teaching on the spiritual life.

Father Robert Faricy, S.J., is ably qualified as a Professor of Spiritual Theology and, indeed, an expert in the area of Ascetical Mystical Theology, having taught these past seventeen years in a major Roman university. Furthermore, Father Faricy has been a leader in the Catholic Charismatic Renewal during the past fifteen years and has served until recently as a spiritual director to the Italian National Service Committee. In the past six years, Father Faricy has also specialized in the phenomena of Marian apparitions, visions, and locutions.

I know the author and have benefited from his passionate devotion to know what God is doing and saying and to follow it. This zeal brings a special dynamic note to this presentation.

Simply, yet profoundly, Father Faricy gives us a book of great significance to scholars and great assistance to people serious about the spiritual life. He cross-relates and gives practical application to traditional teachings in ascetical mystical theology and contemporary experiences of today's Catholic, particularly regarding the charismatic renewal.

The book is not new, having been published earlier as part of a series. It is like good wine well tested. It will be fruitful in the lives of all readers.

The first part of the book is consistent, solid, and integrated. Traditional ideas on contemplation are synthesized with contemporary emphasis on a personal relationship with Jesus, being baptized in the Spirit, and praying in tongues.

Father Faricy knows his material and evidences his scholarship as a Professor of Spiritual Theology at the Gregorian University in Rome. He develops yet simplifies for us Ignatian prayer, Teresa of Avila's four stages of prayer and seven mansions. He treats locutions, visions, touches, and dark night of the soul with the same directness and simplicity as he teaches on meditation and praying the rosary.

In the second half of the book, Father Faricy teaches on discernment, relating it primarily to its base in contemplation. He presents the Ignatian rules for discernment as well as insightful guidelines for daily decision making. He briefly treats the related areas of consolations and spiritual warfare. Finally, he focuses all discernment on love.

In these latter areas, the reader will sense that there is much more to be developed and that the author is well equipped to meet the task. As you finish this book, you will be ready for the next which we all trust is coming.

Father Michael Scanlan, T.O.R.
August 1, 1987

1

PERSONAL RELATIONSHIP
WITH JESUS CHRIST

Jesus Christ, God become human for me, has died on the cross, risen from the dead, and ascended to the right hand of the Father as Lord of the universe and as my personal Lord. The Lord of all is, at the same time, the Lord of my life.

Jesus risen calls me by name. He knows me perfectly, through and through, good and bad qualities, past, present, and future. He accepts me entirely, loves me completely exactly as I am in all my weakness and smallness and sinfulness. And he calls me by name to himself.

Called by Name

Whatever my state of life, whatever my personal vocation—whether I am single or married, a dentist or a housewife or a salesperson, living alone or with others—

fundamentally I am called by the Father to union with his Son Jesus and with the Father in the unity of the Holy Spirit. This is my basic and most fundamental personal vocation. Whatever else God calls me to is a variation, a further detailing, of my basic vocation: union with him, now and in the world to come. "You have made us for yourself," Augustine prayed, and I can say with him to God, "and our hearts shall find no rest until they rest in you."

"God . . . chose us in him [in Jesus Christ] before the foundation of the world, that we should be holy and spotless before him, destining us in love to be his adopted children through Jesus Christ" (Ephesians 1:3-5). I was, before I existed, called to be—called to be created—in and through Jesus Christ (John 1:1-2). I exist because the Father has called me to exist in and through Jesus, and to grow in union with Jesus. This is why I exist, the meaning of my life: union with Jesus Christ.

God's personal call to me, my personal vocation ("vocation" means "call") from him, is even more basic than my existence. Only God exists by his own power. I exist by God's power, by the power of his love which calls me by name. God has called me into being, and he calls me to grow in his Son Jesus.

This is who I am: this particular person called by God to growing union with Jesus Christ. I do not yet fully know who I am. Things and persons are known in their true identity only by the way they turn out in the end. I am becoming my true self, who I really am. I will not find out until after I have died and gone to the Lord who I really am; my true and deepest identity lies hidden in him. After my life on earth, he will give me "a white stone" with my "new name," my secret and true name, written on it (Revelation 2:17).

The full meaning of myself will be revealed to me only at the end of my personal history in this life. Because: the authentic meaning of anyone is revealed only by and in what that person finally turns out to be. And this, at least in part, is the significance of Jesus' parable of the workers who arrive at the eleventh hour (Matthew 20:1-16) and the conversion of the good thief on Calvary (Luke 23:40-43). I am oriented toward my final fulfillment in Jesus. I can find my meaning and direction only in him. This is what I mean when I say that Jesus is the Lord of my life.

And, further, this is what is meant by creation in Christ. All things are created in Christ, and so therefore am I. Everything holds together in him, is created in him (Colossians 1:16-17), is relative to him. And so am I. My true and secret self is: myself-in-relation-to-Jesus.

I am God's "product, created in Christ Jesus" (Ephesians 2:10). And the meaning of my life is to grow in union with, in interpersonal relationship with Jesus Christ, in friendship with him.

Growing in union with Jesus, I become more my true self, the real me. His love continues to create me, to renew me, to make me more myself.

Love Personalizes

A union differentiates the united elements. We can see that in the human body; the various organs and parts are highly developed and highly differentiated because they perform different functions. So too on a team: a teaching team or a surgical team is made up of members who do different things; they are differentiated according to their role on the team. A basketball team's five players have highly differentiated roles; the team works, has a winning unity, precisely to the degree that each player does well his own (differentiated) part.

When a union among persons has not a functional goal in mind, such as teaching or performing surgery or winning the basketball game, when the union is between persons as persons, then the persons are differentiated *as persons*. They are personalized. What unites persons as such, as persons? Love, in one form or another. Married love, family love, love of friendship, all unite persons heart to heart, in and by love. Union of love personalizes the persons united. A married couple, when the marriage is grounded in love and the sacrifice love calls for, does not fuse the two people into one amorphous mass. On the contrary, husband and wife grow as persons not in spite of their daily lived-out union but because of it. Where there is real love in a family, then the members of that family grow as individualized persons precisely in terms of the personalizing union of family love. True friendship, when it avoids possessiveness and manipulation, when it is based on love and not on selfish interest, helps the friends to grow as persons because it is a personalizing union.

So, too, my union with Jesus Christ. The great saints— Francis of Assisi, Teresa of Ávila, Ignatius Loyola, Thomas More, Catherine of Siena, Thérèse of Lisieux, and others— have also been outstanding persons. Their close intimate union with the Lord personalized them, made them more themselves, their true selves. Union of love is not destructive;

it personalizes. And loving union with Jesus Christ personalizes the most.

Relationship with Jesus Christ

The Lord Jesus calls me by name into a close interpersonal and personalizing union of love with himself. Since he is the fulfillment of my whole existence and meaning, then the central relationship in my life should be my relationship with him. My personal relationship with Jesus should be the organizing principle of all my other relationships—with the people I live with, with the other members of my family, with my friends, with the people I work with. My central relationship with Jesus Christ can and should give to the other relationships in my life, especially to the most important ones, life and vitality and meaning, supporting those relationships and helping them.

My relationship with Jesus Christ follows the general laws of all interpersonal relationships, and especially the law that calls for some kind of presence in order for a relationship to exist and to endure. The Lord is always present to me. I have to make myself present to him in a conscious way. When I do that, I am praying. At the center of my life stands my relationship with the Lord. At the center of that relationship is my prayer.

Objectively, I am already in relationship with Jesus Christ. I depend on him, objectively, for my very existence. Prayer means turning consciously to the Lord. Prayer means making my objectively real relationship with the Lord subjectively conscious. It means bringing into my awareness the fact of that relationship.

In prayer, I let my true self come to the surface, emerge. My true self, the real me, is this particular person-in-relation-to-Jesus-Christ. My true and authentic self *includes* my relationship with the Lord. That relationship is more important than the fact that I exist, because any existence depends on my relation to him. Who am I? This particular person-in-relation-to-Jesus. In prayer, I become conscious of, aware of, that fact. That is what prayer is: conscious awareness that I stand in the Lord's presence.

This is a great mystery — that I can actually enter into an intimate, loving, conscious relationship with God-present-for-me in Jesus Christ risen and calling me by name. It is above all a mystery of God's love for me. In his love for me, he sends me his Holy Spirit so that I can pray.

*

Prayer

Lord Jesus, teach me to pray, to enter into loving interpersonal relationship with you. Teach me to come into loving awareness of your great love for me, of the fact that you call me personally, by name, into an intimate and loving union with you.

Teach me to be conscious of my complete dependence on you and on your love for me. Help me to be aware that you are my fulfillment and my future, that the meaning of my life lies in you.

Jesus, teach me to pray. *Amen.*

2

CONTEMPLATION: LOOKING AT JESUS

Jesus' teaching on prayer in Luke's gospel has, as a kind of preface, the story of Jesus' visit to the two sisters: Martha and Mary. Martha, the owner of the house and the one who receives Jesus, complains to him while serving dinner, "Lord, do you not care that my sister has left me to serve alone? Tell her to help me." The Lord answers, "Martha, Martha, you are anxious and bothered about many things; only one thing is necessary; Mary has chosen the better part, and it will not be taken away from her" (Luke 10:38-42). What is the "better part" that Mary has chosen? Mary sits at Jesus' feet, looking at him with love.

Knowledge through Love.

Contemplation means looking at the Lord with love. Contemplation is a way of knowing; I can know the Lord through contemplation—not the way I know data or facts or some truth, but the way I know a person. Through contemplating Jesus, I come to know him better—not to know more about him through study, but to know *him* better through love.

The knowledge of the Lord that comes through contemplation is real knowledge, not less than knowing facts, but more. To know a *person* differs from knowing *about* that person. I do want to know as much as I can about who loves me and whom I love. But beyond that I want to know the person better. Jesus knows me perfectly, accepts me totally, loves me intensely and calls me by name. And he leads me to love him, and to know him better through love—through his love of me and through my loving response to his love.

Knowledge through love, then, is not abstract. The knowledge through love that comes from and that constitutes contemplation is often obscure, dark, vague, shadowy. But not abstract. Contemplation means concrete knowing, because contemplation is lovingly knowing a person, this particular person, Jesus present for me here and now.

Contemplation is an experience of Jesus, of his presence and love and care—not only, nor primarily, intellectual experience, but affective experience, of the heart. Contemplation is affective knowledge, a knowing that takes place through being loved by Jesus and through loving him back.

Feelings, then, count. Sometimes, of course, I can and must pray in dryness in a kind of desert, without any special feelings and perhaps feeling out of touch with the Lord. However, ordinarily, my contemplating Jesus will involve me to some extent at a feeling level, and I will have the spiritual taste that comes with love.

I can expect my contemplating Jesus, my sitting at Jesus' feet and looking at him with love, to have a certain congruency, a fittingness, with my own temperament and nature. Contemplation's knowledge through love is with and according to my whole being, my entire self, my own personal nature. Because it is through love, and because love is an act not just of my will but of my whole person, contemplation is with and through my whole nature, co-operating with my nature, co-natural or connatural. This connatural knowledge is mine, my particular knowing, and so it will have my personal stamp, the quality of my own personality. I do not have to turn into someone else to contemplate Jesus; I do not have to change my personality. The only self I have to relate to Jesus with is the self that I am now. Come as you are.

Contemplation is a grace, a seed that can fall on hard ground, or get choked off with thorns and brambles, or be eaten by the birds, or fall into fertile ground, develop, grow, and bear fruit. In other words, I need to cooperate with the grace of contemplation.

What are the conditions of contemplation? Two. The first is that the grace be given. The second is that I cooperate with that grace.

How can I cooperate with the gift of contemplation? In faithfulness, in freedom, and in simplicity.

Faithfulness.

Through his gift of contemplation, the Lord calls me to faithfulness to him. He calls me to fidelity to a certain substantial amount of time every day spent just being with him, looking at him with love. And my fidelity to time-with-him is really fidelity to him, faithfulness in responding to him calling me by name. There is, certainly, more to contemplation than just putting in the time. Time is a necessary but insufficient condition of contemplation. I have to be there. That is not enough, but it is necessary.

Time is, in this world, a primary expression of commitment, of faithfulness, whether to a project, a cause, an apostolate, or a person. If I am committed to the Lord, I put in time for prayer, an hour a day, or at least a half hour.

But is it sufficient to frequently or usually give a substantial period of time to contemplation? No. It is not enough. The Lord is not a timekeeper. It is not the time in itself that matters, but time as a measure of the quality of commitment, time as a measure of the quality of love. If I am committed in love to Jesus, then I spend time with him regularly, daily; and I let nothing interfere with that, I put nothing in his place or ahead of him in my heart.

Faithfulness, lived out, takes the first step of putting in time.

Freedom

Contemplation calls for an undivided heart. It calls for the interior freedom that comes from putting the Lord first in my life. I need, then, to be free from what we used to call "inordinate attachments." The Lord wants my whole heart, undivided. This does not mean that I should not love other people or that I should not be attached to my work, to my community, to my friends and my family. It means freedom not from all attachments but from inordinate attachments, from the attachments that lead me away from the Lord.

Distractions in contemplation are a clue to my inordinate attachments. If I have a real distraction (not a fly buzzing, or the coldness of my room), something or someone on my mind, that can be a clue. If I am trying to look at the Lord with love but find myself distracted instead by the thought of my friend whom I love, or someone who has hurt me, or the job I have to do, or the fact that I am not adequately appreciated, then I know I have a problem. The content of that distraction indicates an obstacle in my life to contemplative loving union with the Lord.

The Lord calls me to interior freedom. To love my friend not possessively but with an open hand, leaving the friend free from my manipulation and needs and self-gratification. To forgive whoever has hurt me and to be reconciled in my heart with that person. To trust in the Lord for the job I have to do, and to depend wholly on him for the results because, after all, it is his work. To renounce my excessive need for attention and appreciation and narcissistic feedback, and to walk in humility and in service of others. Anything less will block me in contemplation.

On the other hand, putting my inordinate attachments completely in the Lord's hands in my prayer, and then continuing to just look lovingly at the Lord will help me to grow in interior freedom. It will help to straighten out, to put in good order, what remains inordinate in my relationships with other persons, with my work, with myself.

Freedom, lived out, takes the form of an undivided heart.

Simplicity

The Lord calls me to receive the Kingdom like a little child. The Kingdom is his heart, and he offers me his heart in my contemplative prayer. I want to receive it—not in a childish way but in a *childlike* way, simply. Psychologists have determined that the appropriate behavior for an adult in an intimate love relationship is childlike behavior. Contemplation is the intimate expression of an important love relationship in my life. i can and should act in a simple and childlike way.

Martha acted in a quite adult way with Jesus, with great responsibility, with competence, busy about many things, taking care of Jesus, doing a good job. Mary, childlike, sat at Jesus' feet and looked a him with love, simply; contemplation does that. Simplicity in prayer takes shape as quiet attentiveness.

I cooperate with the grace of contemplation by responding to Jesus faithfully, freely, simply.

*

Prayer

Lord Jesus, increase in me your gift of contemplation. You have said, "Ask and you shall receive, seek and you shall find, knock and it will be opened to you." I am asking you for a new and great outpouring of the grace of contemplation. I seek you, your face, to be able to look at you with love. I am knocking, knowing your opening the door further for me means giving me more fully the gift of intimate loving contemplative union with you.

Mary, mother of Jesus, pray for me for the grace of contemplation. And pray for me that I may be faithful to your son Jesus through fidelity to daily prayer. Pray that I may be free and stay free, my heart centered on Jesus, living for him. Pray that I may receive his love and his grace with the simplicity of a child, taking seriously Jesus' love for me, not questioning it but accepting it simply and responding in a simple way, but just looking lovingly at him. *Amen*

3

CONTEMPLATION: GIFT OF THE SPIRIT

In a future-oriented culture like the general occidental culture we share today, pragmatism tends to govern our interests. We take pragmatic interest in whatever helps us to cope with the future. We look for "how-to-do-it" answers rather than search for the meaning of things. Hence the contemporary predominance of technology. Technology is "know-how." If I can just learn the way it is done, I will be all right. For example, how can I pray? What technique will help me? Zen? Yoga? Rhythmic breathing? Keeping a journal? Repeating a mantra? If only I can make the right workshops, find the guru who will help me, keep stabbing at it until I push the right button.

Christianity stands for the primacy of the interpersonal

over the technical, the technological, the "way to do it." Like western culture, eastern religions tend to stress technique, ways to get things done, methods. Eastern religions tend to specialize in prayer techniques, in spiritual technology. So, in our technological age, many who look for God or for some kind of religious experience turn to the techniques of eastern religions to find out "how to" find God. They fill workshop rosters, going from one technique to the next, like the woman who had consulted all the doctors but got no relief. Finally, she reached out and touched Jesus, and he healed her. Contemplation touches Jesus.

Contemplation is not so much what I do as what the Lord gives me. Contemplation is a gift, his gift to me, a gift of his Spirit. I can dispose myself to receive the gift of contemplation and to grow in that gift; but even such a disposition comes from the Lord, is grace. No technique can achieve or win contemplation.

The way to dispose myself to receive the gift of contemplation and to grow in the gift is *not* to look for, yearn for, strive for contemplation. It is, rather, to look for, yearn for, strive for Jesus. In his own time and way, he will give himself to me through increasing graces of contemplation.

Christian contemplation is not technique. It is interpersonal relationship—relationship with God present to me and for me here and now in Jesus Christ. It differs radically from zen contemplation and from all types of buddhist contemplation, as well as from yoga contemplation and transcendental meditation, because it centers on the Lord, on a person. It is essentially a loving relationship.

Centering Prayer

This is where so-called "centering prayer" differs from the use of a mantra. A mantra, a word or phrase concentrated on and repeated over and over, is not interpersonal. Centering prayer centers not on a word or phrase, such as the name of Jesus, but centers through a word or phrase on the person. Repeating the name, "Jesus," over and over slowly, not with my lips but silently in my heart, I center on the person whose name I say in my heart, on the person my heart calls and rests in.

Or I can use the "Jesus prayer," the "prayer of the pilgrim": "Lord Jesus Christ, have mercy on me, a sinner," repeating the phrase over and over silently in my heart. But the focus here is on the Lord Jesus Christ, not on a technique. This way of praying, to repeat in one's heart an ejaculation or the name of Jesus, is—surely—a good way to pray; it can lead to real contemplation. But contemplation itself, that mysterious and conceptless interpersonal encounter with Jesus Christ, remains his gift, his to give, and mine to receive—not to conquer or to achieve through technique, nor to somehow win or merit.

Contemplation and the Gift of Tongues

Why is it that so many men and women have found that the Baptism in the Spirit has given them a whole new relationship with the Lord in prayer? Why have so many found that participation in the charismatic renewal, particularly through receiving the Baptism in the Spirit and the gift of praying in tongues, has led them for the first time to real contemplative prayer or has led them to a new and deeper contemplation? It seems clear that the great grace of the charismatic renewal is a renewed interpersonal relationship with Jesus Christ in personal prayer, a breakthrough in contemplative prayer. Why?

For one thing, of course, the Baptism in the Spirit is a great grace and marks an outpouring of graces and gifts. For another, the gift of praying in tongues is, itself, a gift of contemplative prayer. To receive the gift of praying in tongues *is* to receive a gift of contemplation. Obviously, this can and does carry over into personal prayer in the form of a deeper silent contemplation.

In my experience of spiritual direction, I have found the gift of tongues to be the single biggest help toward contemplative prayer, because the gift of tongues is a type of contemplation. When I contemplate silently, I look—with the eyes of faith— at the Lord, without meditating, without concepts. Contemplation in silence is a non-conceptual prayer, a conceptless looking with love at the Lord.

Praying in tongues is, also, a non-conceptual prayer, a conceptless looking with love at the Lord. When I speak or sing in tongues, I do not speak or sing a language, at least not in the vast majority of cases. Scientific analysis of tapes of tongue-speaking has never found the structure of a real language. When I pray in tongues, I babble; linguistically, I am saying or singing gibberish. The meaning is not in the sounds, as though they were words that represented concepts. The meaning of prayer in tongues lies in the heart, because prayer in tongues is non-conceptual. The sounds are not words; they have no conceptual meaning. They are just meaningless syllables.

Praying in tongues is vocalized non-conceptual prayer. It is noisy contemplation.

There is an analogy between praying in tongues and saying the rosary in such a way as to contemplate the mysteries of the life of Jesus while saying the words. When I say the rosary, I "meditate" on the various mysteries; in reality, I look at— contemplate—Jesus or his mother in the different mysteries. I say the words, but I pay no attention to their meaning; my attention is not on the words I say but on the Lord at whom I am looking. The words might as well be just sounds. Praying in tongues is similar; I pay no attention to the nonsense syllables I am saying or singing because I am looking at the Lord, contemplating him.

Many people who have the gift of tongues begin their daily personal prayer with a brief period—perhaps thirty seconds or a few minutes—of praying in tongues. In that way, they enter consciously into the Lord's presence; they enter easily into contemplative prayer and then remain there silently.

The principal use of the gift of tongues is not, as many suppose, in prayer groups or in charismatic conferences. It is in personal prayer (1 Corinthians 14:2-4). I know several people who have no contact with the charismatic renewal movement and who have never felt called to it, but who regularly pray in tongues in their personal prayer. The gift of tongues is for everyone, not only for those in the charismatic movement.

But is it not necessary to be prayed over for the Baptism in the Spirit to receive the gift of tongues? No. Some pentecostal churches hold that Baptism in the Spirit is a necessary prerequisite for the gift of tongues. Catholics do not hold this. The gift of tongues had no pre-conditions. "Ask, and you shall receive."

True, in classical pentecostalism and in the charismatic renewal in the mainline Protestant churches and in the Catholic Church, the gift of tongues has become a kind of cultural badge, a way of identifying with the group, a sociological sign of belonging. This is not all bad. Since praying in tongues involves enough humility and interior freedom to let go of control of what one says and just let it flow up from the center of one's being, since praying in tongues requires that one risk looking and sounding foolish in the eyes of the world, it helps us to be free from excessive desire for esteem. It helps keep out of the charismatic renewal any who might want to be in it for reasons of prestige. There is no prestige in having the gift of tongues.

On the other hand, the gift of tongues should not be a sociological badge of belonging. It is a gift of contemplation. And you do not have to belong to charismatic renewal or to anything else to receive the gift of tongues. It is not the property of the charismatic movement, nor of any movement. It belongs to Christianity, and any Christian can receive it.

How Can I Receive the Gift of Tongues?

If the gift of tongues is not necessarily tied to prayer groups or to the charismatic movement or to the prayer for the Baptism in the Spirit, and if it will help my personal prayer and lead me to a more contemplative experience of the Lord, then I want it. How can I get it? Not by any technique. But how then can I receive the gift of tongues? By asking the Giver.

Go to your room or somewhere where you can be alone, kneel down, and ask the Lord to give you the gift of praying in tongues. Then, with faith in him and his goodness, look at him with the eyes of faith. Open your mouth, and begin to sing or to say syllables to him, syllables that make no sense, like a baby that has not yet learned to talk. Then let it flow. If you find yourself making strange sounds to the Lord, then you are praying; that is the gift of tongues. The uncomfortableness you feel is your pride hurting; you will get over that.

Then thank the Lord for the new gift of contemplation he has given you.

*

Prayer

Lord Jesus, thank you for all the gifts of prayer you have given me in the past and that you intend to give me in the future. I accept your gifts of prayer. I do not want to refuse any gift that you might want to give me. Help me to open my heart to an increase of the gifts you have given me and to any new gifts you want to give me now.

Teach me to cling to you, to hold close to you, to be far more attached to you, the Giver, than to any of your gifts.

Help me not to kick against the goad when you allow my prayer to lie in darkness and dryness. Give me the grace to remain calm and at peace with you in the dark as well as when the light of your love brightens my prayer. Teach me to walk in prayer lovingly with you in the desert as well as in the garden of consolations.

Increase in me, Lord, you gift of contemplation. Let me always keep the eyes of my heart fixed on you. I ask you this through the intercession of your mother. *Amen.*

4

CONTEMPLATING JESUS IN THE MYSTERIES OF HIS LIFE

Contemplation means looking at the Lord with love. I can look at Jesus in the context of his life on earth; I can contemplate him saying and doing and undergoing the things he said, did, underwent, as the gospels describe his life, death and resurrection.

Ignatian contemplation

Saint Ignatius Loyola, in his *Spiritual Exercises*, gives us a way to look at Jesus in the various "mysteries" (that is, the different events) of his life. Ignatius suggests that, after I reverently acknowledge the Lord's presence, I make three brief "preambles" before I settle down to the activity of contemplation.

The first preamble is to read a gospel text, perhaps—for example—the gospel of the day. For the second preamble, after closing the Bible, I briefly try to imagine the situation of the text, I try to picture it in my imagination seeing Jesus and those around him speaking and acting, imagining the physical conditions—whether outside or in a room, and so on. In the third preamble, I ask for the grace that I want: to know Jesus better so as to love him more and to follow him more closely. All this takes just a few minutes, and has as its purpose to help me to enter into the contemplation of the selected gospel passage.

The question is: now what? What do I do after the preludes, after I am all set? Some people have been taught to *meditate* on the gospel passage. I learned to think about what I had read and imagined in the preludes, to ask myself a series of questions: Who is present? What are they doing? What are they saying? To whom? Why? When? Where? I may have been taught to apply what I had just read to my own life, asking: What does this say to me? How does this apply to me here and now? Some of us were led, by the Lord or through reading or instruction, from simple discursive meditation to affective prayer. That is, I talked to the Lord about the gospel text, asked *him* what it meant for me and how it applied to my life. I talked to Jesus risen, present now, loving me, about what I had read and imagined. And this talking-to-the-Lord some- times led me to acts of faith, hope, trust, love, sorrow for sin.

This is, in itself, a good way to pray. It does not seem to me, however, to cover all that Ignatius Loyola proposes in his *Spiritual Exercises* concerning how to pray about the mysteries of the life of Jesus. Ignatius, telling us how to go about making the "contemplations" on the life of Christ, seems to present not one method but a broad spectrum of several overlapping approaches that flexibly leaves lots of room for the individual differences of those doing the "contemplations." In other words, the term "contemplation" has for Ignatius a quite broad meaning. It includes meditation, praying in one's own words, affective prayer, and contemplation properly so called. I can, then, make a kind of meditation on, for example, the mystery of the presentation of the infant Jesus in the temple, imagining the persons, actions, place, words, and reflecting on them to my own profit, ending my meditation by talking to the Lord in a colloquy using my own words, and for instance, repeating the third prelude by asking to know, love and follow Jesus more. So doing, I would remain faithful to what Ignatius proposes in the *Exercises*.

On the other hand, on the same Ignatian spectrum, I can find room for a quite different approach to praying about a given gospel passage—for example, the Presentation. The "contemplations" on the life of Christ can be approached in a strictly contemplative perspective. In this chapter, I want to consider contemplating Jesus in the mysteries of his life as contemplation strictly speaking. From here on, then, in this chapter, by *contemplation* I mean a gift, divinely given as a special grace, of somehow looking at the Lord with the eyes of faith, in hope and in love, with few or no words or concepts.

The Grace of Contemplation

Not uncommonly, one finds people who stick to a meditative and "busy" approach to praying, using a gospel passage for their daily period of quiet time with the Lord, and wondering why their prayer remains so dry and distracted and unsatisfactory as well as unsatisfying. Often the reason is this: the person has long ago outgrown discursive prayer, has been led by the Lord beyond meditation, beyond reflection, to a prayer of simple regard, to a contemplative prayer. But he or she insists on praying the way they were taught. If the Lord gives me graces of contemplative prayer and I, even without meaning to, insist on being a Martha-busy-about-many-things such as reflecting, applying, and making acts of the will of various kinds, then I will be like someone trying to rhumba with a partner who is doing a slow waltz. Prayer, in fact, is analogous to dancing. And the one who leads is the Lord. If I do not follow his lead, I will find myself doing my own step alone in a desert of dryness and dissatisfaction.

How can I approach a gospel text in a contemplative way? How can I contemplate Jesus in the mysteries of his life? How can I cooperate with the contemplative graces the Lord gives me, cooperate in an intelligent way with at least some understanding of what I do?

A Contemplative Approach to the Life, Death, and Resurrection of Jesus

Ignatius Loyola's three preludes are, it seems to me, useful and important in truly contemplating the Lord as he is presented in the gospels. Even more important, I think, is some kind of prayer of the presence of God at the very beginning of the time for prayer. Many people begin their prayer by praying in tongues for some seconds or for a few minutes, either aloud or under their breath depending on the situation. This puts them right into close contact with the Lord. After that, I can quickly make the three preludes, reading the gospel text (today's gospel, for example), imagining the scene briefly without straining or working my imagination hard, and asking Jesus for what I want: *to know him better*, so that I can love him more and follow him more closely.

Now we are back to the question asked earlier in this chapter: What do I do after the preludes, when I am all set? The key to contemplation is not to do something, but to just look at the Lord and let him do whatever he wants, to look at the Lord and to let him love me the way he wants to love me at the moment—in total silence or showing me something or simply making me aware of his presence. And the key to contemplating the Lord in a gospel passage is not that I remember what Jesus said or did, but that *Jesus remembers*.

Jesus remembers, and he is present, risen, here with me in my prayer to take me into his memory, to let me share his memory of what the gospel text describes. To use an image that is also a reality, I can let Jesus take me into the wound in his side, to his heart. Risen, Jesus still carries the five wounds of his crucifixion and death in his glorified body, the very wounds themselves glorified. I can let him lead me right to his heart, and to share the memory of a particular gospel passage as that memory exists now in his heart. I can rest there, letting him quietly and gently draw me into the essence of his memory of what he did, of what he said, of what he underwent. I can let Jesus lead me to where I can rest in his heart, at the still point of the deepest meaning of the gospel passage.

I might use centering prayer, repeating his name in my heart, very slowly, "Jesus. . . . Jesus. . . . Jesus." I can contemplate—*see*—the event, but in a dim, vague, obscure way, with the eyes of pure faith. Or I can let the Lord use my imagination turned over to him, let him show me and let me listen to what happened by using my imagination to give me the picture. It is a question not of the external senses but of the interior senses, especially of a certain relish, a tasting the mystery interiorly.

However the Lord chooses to lead me in contemplation, I want to be quiet and to let him lead. Even if it seems that nothing is happening, he is with me, here, and that is what matters.

Contemplation and the Rosary

Can saying the rosary be contemplative prayer?

When I pray the rosary, I do not have to think about the words of the prayers that I say. I can repeat the prayers in a kind of automatic way without thinking about the words that I say, without referring in my mind to the intellectual content of the prayers. My hands hold the beads and my mouth says the words, but my mind—and my heart—are on the particular mystery. If, for example, I say the fourth decade of the joyful mysteries, I pray about the fourth joyful mystery, the presentation of Jesus in the temple. In fact, I look, with the eyes of faith, and with love, together with the mother of Jesus, while I say the prayers, at the infant Jesus in the mystery of his presentation in the temple.

But is this really contemplative prayer? Certainly it can be. At the least, looking at Jesus in the various mysteries while saying the rosary is a good way to dispose oneself for the grace of infused contemplation, for the divinely given gift of contemplation. And, of course, many people who say the rosary regularly do engage in contemplative prayer. There are people who have never known any kind of regular prayer except the Mass and the rosary, and whom the Lord has led to highly contemplative prayer exercised by participating in the Mass and by saying the rosary.

*

Prayer

Lord Jesus, teach me to pray. Teach me to pray not with many words, but with my heart.

Give me your Holy Spirit of love so that I can know you through love and, knowing you better, love you more and follow you more closely. Fill me with the grace of your Holy Spirit of light so that I can look on your face with the eyes of faith. Pour into my heart the power of your Holy Spirit; empower me to stay with you in peace, contemplating you in love, knowing you in the darkness of faith.

You have closely examined me, Lord, and you know me. You know my sitting and my standing up and my lying down. You know all my thoughts. You know perfectly all my ways, every path I take. You know what I will say before I say it. You are behind me and ahead of me. Knowing this is too much for me, too high. Where could I go, Lord, to flee from your Spirit or from your presence? (Psalm 139:1-7).

Jesus, you are with me here, teaching me to pray. You know me through and through; you love me and accept me totally; you take me to yourself. Teach me to take seriously your knowledge of me and your love for me. Teach me to respond to you, to know you and·to love you. Teach me to pray.

I ask you this through the intercession of your mother, Mary. *Amen.*

5

CONTEMPLATING JESUS PRESENT IN MY LIFE

Jesus Christ came into this world, died, rose from the dead, and ascended into heaven not only to sit at the Father's right hand but also to be present to this world in a new way: as Lord.

Paul's letters to the Ephesians (chapters 1-3) and the Colossians (chapters 1 and 2) describe Jesus' lordship, his sovereignty, over all things and all persons, over everything and everyone. Jesus' universal sovereignty makes him the Lord of all, so that "every knee must bow and every tongue confess that Jesus Christ is Lord" (Philippians 2:6). Jesus has a name and title above every other name and title (Philippians 2:5): "Lord." His lordship, however, is not just a name, not only juridical; it is organic, real, effective, and dynamic. "All things hold together in him" (Colossians 1:17) truly and organically. He stands, risen, as the keystone, the lynchpin of everything, holding all things and each thing together in himself. He is Lord.

The Father's plan, revealed to us in Jesus, is to bring all things into a unity, reconciling everything under one head, Jesus. This recapitulation of all under Jesus is what the Father intends; it is the meaning of history.

What holds true for Jesus' lordship over the world holds true for his lordship over me. Jesus is my Lord. I hold together in him. The Father's plan is to bring me, and everything in my life, into a unity in Jesus, reconciling everything in my life by recapitulating it all under one head Jesus. I can cooperate with the Father's plan for me, so that my whole life is centered on and anchored in Jesus, by contemplating Jesus as Lord of my life.

Contemplation and Integration of Life.

Jesus' project for me is the same as the Father's: to get me together by uniting me to himself in love. My prayer of contemplation can be my principal cooperation with Jesus' project for me. I can cooperate with him by simply putting myself and everything and everyone in my life in his hands. Without thinking about whatever might be tugging at my mind during my prayer, I can put it—and leave it—in Jesus' hands, under his lordship.

Distractions in prayer have here a particular importance. Whatever comes into my mind as a distraction—a person I care about, someone who has hurt me, my work, a worry about the future—represents in some way an inordinate attachment, a relationship (of love, or resentment, or to my work or my future) not completely under Jesus' lordship, not yet entirely integrated into my relationship with him. If the relationship indicated by the distraction were fully integrated into my relation to the Lord, it would not appear as a distraction; if it leads me away from him, at least to some extent, in my prayer, then it does that too in my life. Part of my life remains outside his lordship.

What can I do about it? I can put the content of the distraction under Jesus' lordship, into his hands, cooperating with his work of centering all in my life on him. Then, leaving the matter there, without mulling it over or dwelling on it or thinking about it at all, I go on contemplating, looking at Jesus, being quietly with him.

I contemplate Jesus in my life, as Lord of my life, as center of my concerns, as holding my whole self and life and all that my life contains in his hands. What has been tugging at my mind rests safely in his hands.

Jesus is Lord not only of my present, but of my future. He is the Lord of history, and also of my personal history—including my future history. My worries about the future can, when they come up as distractions in my prayer, turn into occasions for a trusting and hopeful looking at Jesus in contemplation. He stands with me in my prayer as the ground of my hope, as the rock of my future. I do not know what the future holds, but I do know that he holds my future in his hands, hidden from me but known perfectly to him. He makes present to me now in himself my future—in dark and hidden way. I hope in him for the future, because he holds—and he is—my future.

When, in contemplation, I turn myself entirely over to the Lord with all my worries, preoccupations, good feelings and bad, then—through my contemplation and quietly in his love for me—he pulls me together, knits up the frazzled and unravelled threads of my life, integrates me by centering me in love on him.

"Lord Jesus, I give myself to you. And I turn over to you my problems, my worries, my feelings, my thoughts and my plans. Be the Center of my life. I want you and choose you to be not only first in my life but central. I choose you as Lord, as my Lord, as Lord of my life.

"Teach me to pray. Give me your peace, the peace that comes from leaving myself and my whole life in your hands with complete trust. Give me the grace of contemplation, of resting quietly in you. Amen."

Contemplation and the Healing of Memories

Jesus is Lord of history, past and present and future. And he is the Lord of my own personal history, not only present and future but also past. The Father chose me in Jesus even before the foundation of the world (Ephesians 1:4) and destined and appointed me to live for the praise of Jesus' glory (Ephesians 1:12). I was chosen in Jesus before I was born; even before I was conceived in my mother's womb I was chosen. Jesus was with me, I in him, chosen in him, from the very beginning of my existence, from the moment of my conception. He has been present to me, with me, watching over me with love, all during my life. He has shared my every moment, all my joys and sorrows, my pain and my hurts, my growing, my gains and my losses.

I can look back and see him in my past life; he was there even when I was not aware of him. Remembering the past, I can invite Jesus into my memories. The importance of inviting Jesus into my memories lies in this: many of my present problems and many of the obstacles to my growing in prayer have their roots in my memories of past hurts and pains. Jesus can remove the obstacles by healing my memories.

This, then, presents me with the possibility of growing spiritually, of being healed in my inner self, by contemplating Jesus in my memories of the past. All of us have been hurt: in our childhood, in adolescence, in our religious formation and afterward. We remember these hurts. Some of them we still carry around inside ourselves. We think we outgrew the pain and that the wounds are healed. But perhaps not.

Perhaps I have not yet completely forgiven the persons who hurt me in the past, my father for his severity or because he drank too much or because he really wanted another kind of child than what I was, my mother for her selfishness or possessiveness or neurotic traits. And perhaps my memories of hurtful past situations or events still contain elements of pain or fear or resentment or anger, or of loneliness or humiliation or feeling rejected.

What can I do about it?

I can invite Jesus into those painful memories. Using my imagination, I can recreate in my mind the past situations, remembering the places, the people, and what went on. And I can see, in my imagination, Jesus present there, in the situation, with me. I can contemplate Jesus, look at him there, seeing what he does, hearing what he might say. I can let him into each hurtful memory so that he can heal it. Jesus wants to heal me by healing my painful memories. He heals them not by making me forget, but by taking out of those memories the negative things that have caused me difficulties: the sorrow, the grief, the hurt, the anger and resentment, the fear, the humiliation, the feelings of rejection. In this way, the Lord changes the meaning of those memories so that I can praise and thank him for all the aspects, even the negative aspects, of my life.

For example, let us say that my mother died when I was still young. I can, in prayer, ask Jesus to take my hand and to lead me back in memory to when my mother died. I can ask him to help me to relive what happened, together with how I felt about my mother's death. I can imagine the home I lived in, the other persons in the family the way they were then, seeing it all in my imagination the way it looked to me when I was that age.

I can, for instance, imagine my mother's wake, see the room where her body was, the casket. And I can invite Jesus into that room, contemplate him there, see him looking at me with love, watch what he does, how he acts. I can let him heal that painful memory.

Forgiveness plays an important role in the healing of memories. Many of my past hurts were caused by persons. Many, in fact, were caused by persons who loved me but who were not perfect and who, to some extent and in one way or another, perhaps unknowingly or in spite of themselves, caused me harm—my parents, for example, my close friends. I may think I forgave the persons who have hurt me, but I need to forgive again and again, seventy times seven.

For example, if my father drank excessively, or was quite strict or cold towards me when I was small, if I perceived him in such a way, even if I was mistaken, that made me afraid of him or resentful towards him, then I can forgive him now in my heart. If he has passed away, I can pray to him, tell him personally that I forgive him. Forgiveness can be difficult in some cases, but I can ask the Lord for the grace to forgive.

I can contemplate Jesus in my act of forgiveness. I can imagine the person who hurt me, as he or she was at the time, and then in my imagination I can put my arms around that person, say, "I forgive you," and see Jesus present putting his arms around both of us, giving me the grace to forgive, reconciling us.

And I can contemplate Jesus in the hurtful situation or event as I remember it in my imagination. I can see him there, loving me and healing me, healing my memory of what happened by entering that memory and taking the hurt out of it.

*

Prayer.

Lord Jesus, I offer you my whole past personal history. You alone understand me perfectly. You alone know perfectly all that has happened to me, all that I have undergone, all that has made me who I am right now.

You alone have the white stone with my secret and true

name written on it; you alone hold the secret of my identity, of who I am. You alone know me perfectly and love me unconditionally and perfectly.

Bring to my mind whatever memories you want to heal. Teach me to take each of those memories one at a time, remembering how it was, and contemplating you in each painful memory. Heal me of my past—or hurts I have suffered, of the consequences of my sins and of the sins of others, of the results of not being shown enough attention or love or respect.

I put myself entirely in your hands with my whole life. Come Lord Jesus. *Amen.*

6

THE TRAJECTORY OF PRAYER

Growth in prayer is this: Jesus draws me into an ever closer union with himself. Progress in prayer means growing in friendship, in intimate loving personal relationship, with Jesus Christ. This process of growth in prayerful union with the Lord has a shape, takes the form of a certain path or trajectory that has a beginning, a middle, and an end. The Christian mystical tradition has discovered a pattern in this process. The Christian trajectory of growth in prayer follows a general curve with certain characteristics.

This "growth curve" or path of prayer begins with prayer that depends to a great extent on reasoning, on thinking, on meditation in the sense of mentally mulling over the faith facts of Christianity: the gospel descriptions of Jesus' actions and teachings, the truths of the faith, the meaning of God in our life. Gradually, this "thinking" or discursive prayer gives way to more affective prayer, to acts of the will by which we adhere to the Lord: acts of love, faith, hope, sorrow for sin, trust, praise, and so on. These acts, in the framework of prayer as a talking to the Lord, over a period of time become more simple, less wordy, more of a loving looking at the lord, more quiet, more contemplative.

The trajectory of prayer continues through stages of contemplation up to the highest kind of union with God. This process of growth in contemplative union with the Lord has been best described by Saint Teresa of Ávila and Saint John of the Cross. In these two chapters, I want to sketch out their doctrine, simplifying and commenting, to give a broad picture of what happens along the path of prayer.

Teresa of Ávila: the Four Waters.

Saint Teresa distinguishes four stages of prayer in her *Autobiography* (tr. E. A. Peers, New York: Doubleday-Image, 1960) and compares them to four ways in which a garden might be watered: by means of carrying water in a bucket, by means of a waterwheel and conduits, by a stream, and by rain.

Beginners in prayer, using vocal or mental prayer, work at their prayer, using much of their own efforts. They find themselves easily distracted, sometimes tempted to give up or cut down on their time for prayer, struggling along in faith. They are watering the garden with buckets of water. The water is consolation, consolation in the sense of facility or ease in relating to the Lord. In the first stage, I need to reason, ponder, make acts of the will, do work, carry the buckets.

In a second stage, I need to do less work in my prayer, which has become simpler, and often takes the form of a prayer of simple regard, a simply being and resting in the Lord's presence. I am using a waterwheel to feed the water into pipes that carry it to the garden.

The "third water" compares a third stage of prayer to having a garden watered by a stream running through it. Prayer here in this third stage is regularly contemplative; the mind and the will have little to do. No real work is needed, because the water flows right through the garden.

The "fourth water" or fourth stage of prayer is a prayer of intimate union with the Lord, of oneness with God. He waters the garden himself with heavy rains.

This simple "four waters" schema, it seems to me, helps us to understand the direction that progress in prayer takes. That direction is one of increasing passivity and of increasing simplicity. I do less as I go along, and the Lord does more. The direction of growth in prayer is towards an increasingly contemplative prayer, of a closer and more intimate union with God. As I move along from one "water" to another, my head and my heart labor less. And finally, in the "fourth water," they rest entirely in the Lord.

The key to understanding Teresa's writing on prayer is, it seems to me, to stay with the images she uses. It seems better to see how the imagery itself, as it is used by Teresa, fits my experience and so helps me to understand it better.

Teresa of Ávila: the Seven Mansions

In the *Interior Castle* (tr. E.A. Peers, New York: Doubleday-Image, 1961) Saint Teresa presents the path of prayer in a description that goes beyond her other writings, including the *Autobiography*, for clarity, for completeness, and for maturity—she wrote the *Interior Castle* at a time of her own life in which she could look back at the path her prayer had taken and see it clearly, as a mountain climber might survey from the mountaintop the path he has taken.

Let us take a quick look at the trajectory of prayer using Teresa's own image, that of an interior (to each of us) castle with seven concentric clusters ("mansions") of rooms; each mansion contains many rooms. Progress in prayer lies in passing from the first outer ring of rooms, the first mansion, to the second, third, and so on until we rest in the seventh and innermost mansion, where the King is. The allegorical castle stands for my own interior self; and so the journey of prayer is an interior one that moves always closer to the closest union with the Lord in the central, seventh, mansion.

The first mansion is for utter beginners in the spiritual life. They have good intentions, but they are so beset with worldly worries and tied down with attachments of various kinds that they are easy prey for the devil. In the second mansion, I have begun to pray regularly; in this mansion, Teresa advises me to do everything I can to conform my will to God's will and to be faithful to prayer.

The third mansion holds some dryness in prayer, but also some felt consolation. Prayer here is quite simplified, and begins to be truly contemplative, inspired by God. Third mansion prayer is the prayer of many good people; they faithfully pray for a good period of time every day, avoid sin, practice virtue. They need, says Teresa, to learn humility. It seems to me that some people, even priests and religious brothers and sisters, somehow get stuck here in the third mansion and never move on. The rigidity of their goodness holds them in a rut; their uprightness keeps them from the lowliness and childlikeness needed to enter the fourth mansion.

The first three mansions of the *Interior Castle* correspond to the first and second waters of the *Autobiography*. The third water, where the stream runs through the garden, corresponds to the fourth, fifth and sixth mansions. The fourth water, rain on the garden, is the same prayer state as the seventh mansion. Many people, it seems to me, judging from my experience, are in the third water, the fourth or fifth or sixth mansion. That is, many people who pray faithfully every day, and who have done so for a number of years, have entered into these mansions, into states of true contemplative prayer. Let us look briefly at mansions four, five, and six.

The fourth mansion is what Teresa names the prayer of quiet. In the prayer of quiet, I experience infused consolations, gladness that comes from the Lord rather than from my own thinking, or — in general — a facility in relating to the Lord that moves me and that comes not from me but from him. The prayer of quiet is not necessarily quiet! Often, it can be painful because of aridity, darkness, or over-activity of a mind and will that refuse to settle down. In fact, a passive purification seems to go with the prayer of the fourth mansion, a darkness that contains distractions, aridity, and of course purification of faith.

Saint Teresa calls the prayer of the fifth mansion the

"prayer of union." In this stage, my prayer is easy. I am centered on the Lord in peace and sometimes in joy. There are times when I am simply there, happy to be with the Lord, caught up in my union with him. This prayer of union seems to be a transition phase; people who enter the fifth mansion do not seem to remain there long, perhaps a few weeks or some months or, in a few cases, about a year.

The "Second Conversion"

The prayer of union of the fifth mansion seems to correspond to a "second conversion" experience.

The idea of a "second conversion" comes from the first few generations of Jesuits in the sixteenth century. A Jesuit's first conversion was supposed to be when he decided to give his life to the Lord and accepted his Jesuit vocation. The second conversion was to take place, according to the Lord's plan and will, some years later. The Jesuit "second novitiate" (also called the "third year of novitiate" or "tertianship") was intended to dispose the Jesuit for his second conversion. The second conversion was marked by new graces of prayer, a new outpouring of apostolic zeal and gifts, and a new level of relationship with the Lord.

In my own work with priests and with religious brothers and sisters, I have found the theory of the second conversion verified. It seems likely that it applies also to those lay persons who lead quite serious spiritual lives. I have found second conversions to occur over a brief time span (anywhere from a few minutes to a week or so) privately, in a person's private prayer, or perhaps unexpectedly. They take place sometimes in directed retreats. Often, most often by far in my experience, they are the result of the prayer for the outpouring of the Holy Spirit (the so-called "baptism in the Spirit") that the charismatic renewal has introduced into the Catholic and other Christian traditions. However and under what circumstances it takes place, this second conversion marks the beginning of something new. It is a re-birth. Prayer becomes easier; the Lord seems near.

In my opinion, often or maybe always, the second conversion marks the entrance into the fifth mansion. This hybrid idea, melding Teresa's prayer doctrine with the Jesuit second-conversion tradition, will not appeal to everyone. But it tallies with my own experience, and I think it is valid. I do not believe that anyone stays long in the fifth mansion. It is a time of consolations, of joy in prayer, a kind of honeymoon with God. It wears off, and the Lord moves me on into the sixth mansion.

The sixth mansion prepares for the seventh, and the preparation can take quite a long time. The sixth mansion is a time of trials, both within and without. There can take place great consolations and special gifts of prayer. Surely, there will be difficulties, both interior and from outside. There can be severe dryness in prayer, for example, coupled with misunderstanding on the part of other persons.

The seventh mansion is the spiritual marriage, a mansion of rest in the Lord, of close intimate union with him. Trials are not over, but the basic peace of such a close union with God remains always; sickness or problems with other persons or other problems are there, but they do not disturb me. I am centered on the Lord.

"*Where am I?*"

The reader may ask himself or herself: "All right, where am I on the charts? What water am I in? In what mansion am I?" For most people, there are several answers to the question, "Where am I on the growth curve, on the trajectory of prayer?" Here are some of them.

It is not at all necessary that I know where I am on the chart, so there is no point worrying about it. It seems to me that most people who have been praying seriously and faithfully every day for several years are in the fourth, fifth, and sixth mansions.

Many people beyond the third mansion just cannot accept that fact. That is all right; there is no need to know where one is, much less to accept the fact.

Some who read Teresa of Avila, her *Interior Castle* for example, misinterpret her. They read about all her special experiences (ecstasy, locutions, and so on) and they think that those paramystical experiences define the stages of prayer in which they happened to Teresa. Not true. The stage of prayer is defined by the *kind* of prayer I have, not by special manifestations. In fact, few people have ecstasies. Not so many have locutions (words from the Lord, heard as though spoken aloud, or heard in the heart, but always with knowledge that the Lord has given them); and, anyway, locutions can occur in any stage of prayer, in any of the seven mansions, not only where Teresa discusses them. Such things do not indicate "where I am" in my prayer. It is a question of how centered on the Lord I am, in my life and in my prayer. I may go all the way to the seventh mansion with few or no unusual experiences in my prayer: no ecstasy, no words from the Lord, no visions—just knowing he loves me and leads me and teaches me to respond.

*

Prayer

Lord Jesus, teach me to pray. Wherever I am along the path you are leading me in my prayer, I am happy to let you love me the way you want to love me at the time, now. You know what kind of prayer I should have now, and you give me that.

Lead me, Lord, and teach me to follow. *Amen.*

7

DARKNESS AND LIGHT

Perhaps most of the time for many people prayer is a desert experience or an experience of darkness. None of Saint Teresa's four waters operates; there is no water. Prayer can be an experience of aridity, of dryness and distraction, or of darkness. This darkness can be full of peace, a restful quiet darkness. It can be painful, like a parching desert. It can get boring. Usually we just have to accept the desert or the darkness, muddling along as best we can, staying faithful, persevering in prayer.

How can I understand this dryness and darkness in my prayer? Is it my fault? What can or should I do about it?

The Dark Night

The heart of Saint John of the Cross's teaching on contemplation is his doctrine of the dark night (*The Ascent of Mount*

Carmel and *The Dark Night*, in *The Collected Works of Saint John of the Cross*, tr. K. Kavanaugh and O. Rodriguez, New York: Doubleday, 1966, pp. 66-389). "Night," for John of the Cross, means "privation," the elimination of all attachments to whatever is not God. The "night" purifies me, empties me of all that is not the Lord. I can be filled with God only to the extent that I am emptied of everything else, purified. Finally my spiritual "eyes" get used to the dark, I learn to "see" in faith, and the dryness and pain of the night move away. The light of the Lord blinds me; it is too bright for me; I perceive it as darkness — until I get used to the dark and I begin to see dimly.

The dark night comes, in one way or another, into the prayer of everyone who prays seriously. It comes in different ways and takes different shapes for different persons. The night is a grace of purification, of getting-empty of what is not the Lord. But I perceive it as darkness, as a sense of the Lord's absence or at least as a lack of feeling his presence. Or I can experience it as dryness, a long hard walk in the desert; or perhaps as a kind of resistance to the Lord and to spiritual things, a dread of God and of my own sinfulness; or as a kind of dull torpor on my part, a fogginess and a helplessness. In this situation, I cannot seem to pray.

The dark night can last a long time, months or, more commonly, years — even several years. Although John of the Cross seems to describe different "dark nights" (the active and the passive nights, the night of the senses, the night of the spirit), he really wants to designate only various aspects (active, passive) of the same night and the successive forms it takes (of the senses, of the spirit).

What causes the dark night in my prayer? My own need

for purification, my own sinfulness, sinful tendencies, selfishness, general unreadiness for the graces the Lord wants to give me as he empties me out, purifies me, by means of the grace of the dark night. Some factor outside myself can act as the occasion, the apparent cause, of the night: a death in the family, a serious failure or rejection, physical or psychological illness, inability to "fit in" with my present situation, outside pressures, loneliness. But the real cause of the night is the Lord working in me, getting me ready, helping me to acquire the "night vision" that I need for greater awareness of him.

What should I do in the night? How do I act in the desert? To begin with, I have to let the Lord love me the way he wants to love me at the time. If I find myself in a night, then I have to accept that fact. The Lord calls me to cooperate with his purifying grace by staying quiet in the dark, with as much peace as I can muster. In particular, he calls me to trust: To trust him, to take seriously his personal love and his care for me, believing he does act in me in secret ways beyond my awareness, knowing that he is the Lord of my life and of my prayer.

The Dark Night and the Mansions

In the first three "mansions" of Saint Teresa of Avila, the grace of the dark night takes the shape of the grace to choose the Lord above all things and to detach myself not only from all sin but also from whatever does not lead me to and unite me to the Lord. John of the Cross calls this part of the dark night "the active night of the senses" — *active*, because *I* do it (with the help of the Lord, of course); *of the senses*, because the purification, the detachment, takes place at the level of the senses, of my feelings. The active part or aspect of the dark night of the senses is, really, a question of love. The love for him that the Lord pours into my heart through his Holy Spirit leads me to choose the Lord, renouncing whatever blocks, or tends to block, my loving choice of him.

The passive aspect of the night of the senses begins with the fourth mansion or, more usually, just before, in the third mansion, with what can be called the prayer of simplicity, or the prayer of recollection, or the prayer of simple regard. Thinking becomes more difficult, slows down to a halt; the acts of faith, hope, love have pretty much merged into a single unified act of reaching out to the Lord. I am no longer at all busy about many things in my prayer. Maybe I feel languid or vacant. I have distractions. I do not know what to do, but I do not feel comfortable doing anything other than just trying to be present somehow to the Lord in my foolish, dull, poor, muddled way.

I have begun — rather, the Lord has begun in me — the passive part of the dark night. He is acting secretly in me, purifying me of my attachment to "satisfaction" in my prayer, emptying me out of my dependence on my own thoughts and feelings in my prayerful relationship with him. It is called "passive" because I receive this purification passively; he does it to me even though I cannot feel what he is doing. I must continue, of course, the active aspect of the dark night. But the more important part is not what *I* do with his help, but what *he* does *in my helplessness*.

This passive side of the dark night can last quite a long time. It can come and go, varying in intensity, fluctuating. It usually comes to an end when I leave the fourth mansion and enter the fifth, when I experience a "second conversion" or some kind of spiritual rebirth after a long time in the prayer of quiet. And then it starts again sometime after I pass from the fifth to the sixth mansion.

The dark night begins again in the sixth mansion; I still need purification. I can experience serious difficulties because of other people's misunderstanding of me or because of other reasons outside myself. And I will experience interior suffering because the Lord will purify my relationship with him even more, emptying me of my attachment to and my dependence on whatever is not the Lord, freeing me also from my dependence on the consolations he gives. This is the dark night of the spirit. It has an active aspect — my active and continuous choosing the Lord above whatever is not the Lord; and a passive aspect — his secret work, in the dark, in me.

Then, when I have become more used to the dark, when I have some "night vision," when the glare of the light of the Lord no longer causes me pain, he leads me into the seventh mansion of resting in him, identified with him, intimately united with him in love.

The doctrine of the dark night can help me to understand what goes on in my prayer, can help me to appreciate the darkness as grace, and can remind me that in and underneath my own felt helplessness in prayer, the Lord works in secret, in the darkness. The Lord also, however, works in the light. He can dazzle me. He can make me feel the warmth of his care and the power of his love for me. He can convert me. He can give me his transforming grace not just in the darkness but also in the light.

In the Light

Contemplative experience varies greatly. The gift of contemplation that the Lord gives varies widely from person to person. Even though we may speak of a general trajectory of prayer, and of the dark night as an experience that comes to all who pray seriously, nevertheless the Lord in his unlimited wisdom gives different gifts to different people — and this is especially true of prayer.

If my prayer is for the most part a dark experience, if nothing special ever happens and I have a difficult time explaining to anyone just what does go on in my prayer, then I am not alone. The experience of praying in faith — knowing the Lord is there without having any convincing evidence of his loving presence, praying without having any truly notable consolations — is not at all an uncommon experience. On the contrary.

However, if the Lord does act in a clearer way in my prayer, or if sometimes, or often, great light comes in my prayer in the form of divinely given insight or understanding, then I must be careful not to confuse the gifts with the Giver. The Lord will sometimes leave me in the desert, without any evidence of his loving presence, and when he does I will grow in dependence on him and in freedom from depending on what is not the Lord — including his gifts to me. The desert, too, is a gift.

Locutions, visions, and similar experiences are not in any way the essence of contemplative prayer. They are helps the Lord gives me if he sees that they will help me. The danger is that I can become attached to them in such a way that he alone is not enough for me; I cannot be happy with him unless he is giving me special gifts all the time. I can get "hooked" on the gifts. The Lord's great gift, and the only one I really need, is the gift of himself.

Saint John of the Cross goes so far as to say that I should not desire visions and locutions and special understanding in my prayer, but I should *desire not to have* them. They are dangerous, even when from the Lord, because I can easily get attached to them in such a way that I am less attached to him.

If the bird is chained to a tree or tied by a thread, it cannot fly. Whether I am tied down by the chain of attachment to serious sin, or whether I am bound by the thread of overdependence on special effects in prayer, I cannot fly: I am not free to belong entirely to the Lord, selfishness taints my love for him.

Some people, and even one or two authors, say or suggest that all such gifts — words from the Lord, visions, gripping consolations — are false, not from the Lord. Some say that they are always or almost always only from the unconscious, and not from God. Those who say such things are wrong; perhaps they lack experience. We want to avoid the errors of both extremes: the error of attaching too much importance to such things and of desiring them, and the error of denying that they can be from the Lord.

On the other hand, I might have, at times in my prayer, "touches" from the Lord, strong and gripping consolations that last only briefly, and I know they are from the Lord. It seems as though he really touches the heart of my soul. These "touches" are not special effects; they are God uniting me strongly to himself. I cannot help but desire that! I *want* to be united to him above all else.

Prayer.

Lord Jesus, teach me to pray. And teach me to let you love me the way you want to love me at this time. Teach me to cooperate with whatever grace you give me, whether that grace gives me joy and gladness or whether it purifies and empties me.

You have said, "Ask and you will receive, seek and you will find, knock and it will be opened to you." I ask you now for the grace to want only you, for the strength and the love of your Holy Spirit in me to keep me always clinging to you, especially in my prayer. Teach me to cleave to you when my prayer is dark, when it is dry and distracted, when I do not experience your love or your presence. And teach me to choose and to cherish you above all things, including the consolations you send me. My God and my all.

I am poor, Lord, and helpless. I sometimes feel like the man going from Jerusalem to Jericho who fell among robbers who left him half dead. My sins and my infidelities and my selfishness have left me half dead. Be to me, Lord, a "good Samaritan" (Luke 10:33-34); have compassion on me. Bind up my wounds, pouring on the oil and wine of your care and your love. Give me the graces of prayer that you see that I need. *Amen.*

8

DISCERNMENT OF SPIRITS: DISCERNING

This chapter discusses the discernment of spirits, especially regarding the contemplative aspect of the discernment. It is about discerning in prayer, as a way of prayer — or, to be exact, as a way of contemplating Jesus.

The reader may notice that the book changes gears at this point. Whereas the chapters on contemplation usually *described* contemplation, those on discernment will give more space to *telling how* to discern. The reason is this: contemplation is a gift, a grace, more what the Lord does in me than what I do; discernment, on the other hand, while also a grace, is also an art. An art can be learned. The purpose of these chapters, and in particular of this one and the two that follow, is to help you to learn the art of discernment. First, however, some distinctions have to be made between various meanings that the term "discernment of spirits" can have.

The Charism of the Discernment of Spirits

The phrase "discernment of spirits" can refer either to a charism or to a general Christian practice. Sometimes, it refers to the *charism* of the discernment of spirits. Saint Paul lists "discernment of spirits" along with some other charisms in his First Letter to the Corinthians (12.10). He writes: "There are varieties of charisms, but the same spirit . . .; to each is given the manifestation of the Spirit for some useful purpose" (1 Cor. 12:4-7). Then he lists several charisms such as healings, working miracles, prophecy, and — among others — the capacity to distinguish between spirits. What is a charism, and what is "the capacity to distinguish between spirits"?

What is a charism? A charism is a special gift or grace that has three characteristics:

1. It is not given to everyone, but only to some people.
2. It is a gift of service, of ministry, "for some useful purpose" (1 Cor. 12:7), for building up the body of Christ which is the Christian community.
3. It is a special relationship with the Lord.

Here are some examples. The gift of consecrated celibacy that Catholic priests and that brothers and sisters of religious congregations have is a charism. Not everyone is called to consecrated celibacy ("Let him take who can take it," Matthew 19:12; "To each his own charism," 1 Cor. 7:7); the charism is given only to some. Secondly, consecrated celibacy frees the priest or nun or religious brother for service of the

Lord (1 Cor. 7:32-35). And thirdly, people who have taken a vow or a promise of consecrated celibacy, including many lay persons, know that this is a special way of belonging to Jesus Christ.

Again, the charism of teaching, especially of teaching Christianity, is given not to all but mainly to those who are called to such a ministry and especially to those who pray for the charism of teaching. It is a gift of service. And it gives the teacher a special relationship to Jesus Christ — as his representative in teaching (see Ephesians 4:11; Romans 12:7). Finally, the Lord gives the charism of evangelization to those called to a ministry beyond the ordinary Christian duty to evangelize, and they have a special relationship with him as evangelizers (see Ephesians 4:11).

The charism of the discernment of spirits is the special gift of grace given to some persons enabling them to tell what things or words or manifestations come from the Holy Spirit, and what does not come from the Holy Spirit but, perhaps, comes even from evil spirits. Most New Testament scholars think that Paul lists the charism of discerning between spirits right after the charism of prophecy because the charism of discernment was used especially for determining which prophecies spoken in the prayer assemblies were really from the Lord —and which ones were not. Perhaps also the charism of discernment was used in exorcisms to discern the presence of evil spirits. And, probably, it was a valued charism in general.

Most of us do not have the charism of the discernment of spirits. And yet, all of us are called to use the discernment of spirits in a more general way, to discern in our own lives what comes from the Holy Spirit and what does not.

The Discernment of Spirits as a Gift for All

The New Testament speaks of the discernment of spirits as a gift for all, not only as a charism but as a gift for every Christian. The few who have the charism will, of course, be stronger in the discernment of spirits than those who do not. Still, we are all called to discern what in our lives comes from the Lord from what does not.

The term "discernment of spirits" as used by Paul in the First Letter to the Corinthians designates the charism. In the First Letter of John, however, "discernment of spirits" means the gift offered to all; all are called to discern: "Beloved, do not believe every spirit, but test the spirits to see if they are of God" (1 John 4:1). And, in fact, even though discernment of spirits is mentioned explicitly only twice in the New Testament, the fact of the discernment of spirits can be found all through the gospels, the Acts of the Apostles, and the rest of the New Testament books. The gospels illustrate the discernment needed to recognize in Jesus the power of the Holy Spirit and the victory over the spirit of evil. Mary discerns the action of God at the Annunciation (Luke 1:35), as does Joseph later (Matthew 1:18-20). Elizabeth and Simeon recognize the Spirit in Jesus (Luke 1:41; 2:26).

Matthew's gospel, in chapters eleven and twelve, shows that underneath Jesus' discussions with the leaders of Israel lies a doctrine of the discernment of spirits. Jesus is the object of this discernment; the presence of the Spirit can be discerned in what Jesus says and does. Understanding Jesus' parables calls for discernment; further, the parables teach discernment — for example, they call us to discern the presence of Jesus in our suffering brothers (Matthew 25:31-46), to be prudent and discerning and not foolish (Matthew 25:14-30), to build on rock and not on sand (Matthew 27:24-25).

Paul practices the discernment of spirits with the various communities to whom he writes. And he preaches discernment (Philippians 1:9-11). Be "led by the Spirit of God" (Romans 8:14); "Walk as children of the light and try to have an interior grasp of what is the Lord's will" (Ephesians 5:8-10; see 5:17). Paul's chief criterion for discernment is a person's relation to Jesus Christ (1 Cor. 12:3; 23:3). The same is true of John's gospel and the letters of John: "By this you know the Spirit of God: every spirit that confesses that Jesus Christ has come in the flesh is of God, and every spirit that does not confess Jesus Christ is not of God" (1 John 4:2-3).

There is a constant Christian tradition of the discernment of spirits from New Testament times to the present. In this tradition, the classic formulation is that of Saint Ignatius of Loyola, the sixteenth-century contemplative and founder of the Jesuits. His rules are unequalled as a practical guide to discernment, and we will follow them for the rest of this chapter.

Discerning the Spirits

Spiritual discernment is that prayerful process by which I examine, through love and in the light of faith, the nature of my experience: does this particular impulse or idea or plan or project or word come from the Lord or not? Is it from the Spirit of Jesus or from some other source? Knowing where a particular thought or plan or word comes from will help me in making decisions; I want to follow up and carry out what comes from the Holy Spirit. And I want to reject and avoid what does not.

Ignatius of Loyola, in his "Rules for the Discernment of Spirits" (*The Spiritual Exercises*, sections 313-336) distinguishes between "good spirits" and "bad spirits." "Good spirits" are the Holy Spirit and angels. Any interior idea or impulse that comes somehow from the Lord, Ignatius attributes to the "good spirit." And any idea or impulse that comes from the traditional sources of temptation — the world, the flesh, and the devil (or the evil spirits that are his minions), Ignatius identifies as from the "evil spirit." The point of the discernment of spirits is this: I want to judge, in a particular concrete instance, whether this idea, thought, plan, impulse, interior urging, comes from the good spirit or the evil spirit.

What criteria do I judge by? What norms do I use for judging my interior experience? I have objective norms and subjective norms. The objective norms exist outside me, go beyond me. The subjective norms are my own conscience and other interior feelings, thoughts, and urgings.

Objectively, the Lord speaks to me, gives me guidelines for living, in the bible, in the doctrines and teachings of the Church, and through whatever legitimate authority I am subject to. So, any idea or impulse I might have, if it seems to contradict my objective norms, needs to be looked at carefully. God does not contradict himself, telling one thing through the bible or the Church and something else in my heart.

Often, the objective norms are insufficient to lead me to a judgment of my idea or feeling. For example, it might very well be an objectively good idea; the question is: is this idea here and now from the Lord for me? The bad spirit might want to lead me to do an objectively good thing at the wrong time, or under unsuitable circumstances, or when I am not the person the Lord wants to do it. In many cases, I need to rely on subjective norms. If my conscience tells me that a certain idea or impulse is wrong, then I know not to follow up on that. But often my conscience does not object. But is this idea or feeling or plan — granted that it is good, not sinful, and objectively feasible — really now from the Lord? How can I tell?

The interior or "subjective" norms that I have for evaluating whether or not this thought or impulse is from the Lord are not subjective in the sense of being arbitrary. They are reliable norms, grounded in the whole objective Christian tradition of the discernment of spirits.

The first norm Ignatius of Loyola gives us is this. If I am moving away from the Lord, living a life of serious sin, then the evil spirit makes me feel good, helps me to find pleasure in whatever leads me further from the Lord. I am moving away from the Lord, and so I find a certain pleasure in ideas and urges that push me to continue in the direction I am already going in. And the good spirit pursues a contrary tactic, causing pain and remorse in my conscience, causing me uneasiness and even anxiety or other negative feelings, because the good spirit is going *against* the direction my life has taken.

On the other hand, if I am trying to lead a Christian life, (and if you are reading this book, you almost certainly are), advancing in the ways of the Lord, then what happens is just the opposite. The evil spirit causes me sadness, uneasiness, fear of obstacles, so as to impede my progress in the Christian direction my life has taken. The good spirit gives me courage, consolations, sorrow and even tears for my sins, inspirations, ease of action in serving the Lord, and a peaceful mind. And that is how I can tell what comes from the good spirit and what comes from the bad spirit: by the results in me.

Ignatius writes: "Persons who are going from good to better the good spirit touches gently, delicately, sweetly, like a drop of water soaking into a sponge; those who are going from bad to worse, the good spirit touches in the opposite way. The reason for this is to be found in the disposition of the person touched, whether he or she is in concord with or contrary to the good or evil spirits touching that person. When the person's disposition is contrary to that of the spirits, they enter with noise and disorder; when it is in concord with the spirits, they enter silently, like someone coming home when the doors are open" (*Exercises*, section 334). Notice that the point here is not *where I am spiritually*, but what *direction* my life is taking. Am I going toward the Lord or away from him?

Consolation

Very often, my best criterion for judging the origin of a thought or a proposed action or an inner urging will be what Ignatius calls "consolation." What does he mean by consolation? I have consolation whenever I begin to be aflame with love for the Lord, when I cannot love anything or anyone on earth except in the Lord and Creator of them all, or when I pour out tears of sorrow for the sufferings and death of the Lord or for my sins or the sins of the world. Or, finally, consolation can be any felt increase of faith, of hope and trust in the Lord, of love, and also every inner gladness that attracts me to the things of the spirit and that brings me interior repose and peace in the Lord. Briefly, a thought or plan or feeling or impulse brings me consolation when it brings me closer to the

Lord, gives me a certain facility in relating to him, in finding him, in being united with him.

For those trying to live a Christian life, trying to live according to the Holy Spirit, consolation is a useful criterion for evaluating interior experience. When I am face to face with the Lord in prayer, looking at him with the eyes of faith and trust and love, how comfortable-with-him do I feel in terms of this particular idea, project, urging? When I contemplate Jesus, offering him this particular thought or impulse, how do I feel in terms of my relationship with him? Do I feel a certain rightness, a certain peace, or perhaps even gladness or joy when I propose this particular thing to the Lord in contemplation? If it gives me what Ignatius calls consolation, then that consolation is a sign that it comes from him.

Ignatius calls "desolation" whatever seems to separate me from the Lord: temptations to sin or to move away from the Lord in any way, gloominess of heart and mind, confusion, whatever causes distrust in the Lord, lack of faith and hope, coldness of love. Briefly, desolation is whatever is contrary to consolation. Is desolation what John of the Cross calls "the dark night"? No. I can, in the dark night of prayer, have either desolation or consolation at different times. The dark night often is, in fact, a time of real peace and rest in the Lord, of being content to be united with him in the dark, and so it is a time of consolation.

Some Rules for Discernment

For one thing, a time of spiritual desolation, a time of feeling somehow distant from God, is no time to change purposes or decisions that were made in times of consolation. If I am tempted to change my good intentions, I can even act in a manner that goes against the temptations, opting, for example, for more prayer, more fasting. In desolation, I can humble myself, learning from the experience how weak and helpless I am and how much I need to depend on the power of the Lord's love for me even when — especially when — I cannot feel it. In desolation, I can hold on in patience, looking ahead to the time when the Lord will again console me.

In times of consolation, I should gather energy for more difficult and perhaps desolate times ahead. And I can humble myself before the Lord recognizing how much I depend on him and how weak and helpless I am without his consolation.

Consolation comes from the Lord and has as its reason my salvation, my greater union with him. Desolation comes ultimately, in one way or another, from the devil, whose strategy is to get me to think I am no good, to hate myself the way he hates me. But why does the Lord allow desolation? What are the reasons for it? There are, Ignatius points out (*Exercises*, section 332), three principal reasons for desolation. First, I might be tepid with regard to my prayer life and my whole relationship with the Lord; as a result of my failings, consolation leaves me. Secondly, the Lord might be putting me to the test, training me in adversity and helping me to build strength the way a coach has a runner run many practice laps to get in shape. Thirdly, the reason for my desolation might be to teach me humility, to help me recognize how little I am by myself, how much I depend on the Lord. Desolation can keep me from building on the sand of my own virtuousness and righteousness and apparently good life; it can strengthen me by leading me to build more securely on the Lord, the rock of my life.

The Problem of Possible Deception

My discernment will not be infallible. It, too, often needs to be discerned, to be monitored, evaluated, and perhaps revised. The problem, as Ignatius puts it, is that the evil spirit can appear as an "angel of light." The evil spirit can first prompt me to have good and holy thoughts and then, little by little, show his true nature by leading me to his own hidden agenda of lies and sin.

Therefore, I have to pay attention not only to the beginning of my ideas, but also to their middle and end. If beginning, middle, and end are completely good and tend toward what is right, then I have a sign of the influence of the good spirit. But if good thoughts end up in something evil or distracting or less good than what I had originally thought of, or if they confuse me or weaken me or take away my peace in the Lord, then I have a sign of the influence of the evil spirit.

But can the evil spirit cause in me consolation, even for his own sinister purposes? Yes and no. Yes in the sense that he can prompt in me good ideas and plans that seem right and good and from the Lord, and then lead me from those thoughts down his own path. He cannot, however, cause consolation that just comes without any adequate previous cause. In other words, if I cannot account for my consolation, either because it just came to me all of a sudden, perhaps together with an idea or insight, or if what led to the consolation is just not enough to provoke such great consolation, then

I can be sure that the consolation is from the good spirit, from the Lord.

Here are examples: many people, when they receive the outpouring of the Holy Spirit in the charismatic renewal (when they receive what is called "the baptism in the Spirit") experience great consolation, joy, strong peace, closeness to the Lord. If this consolation goes far beyond the prayer setting and the excitement of the moment, then they can be sure that the consolation comes from the Lord. Or if, in my prayer, I experience a kind of touch of the Lord, a great surge of love for him that I know is from him, perhaps together with some insight or plan for action, and if the "touch" goes quite beyond what my own prayerfulness could cause, I know that the consolation comes from the Lord.

Can the evil spirit come to me as an angel of light even in the case of consolation without an adequate cause? Yes. He can sneak in afterwards with apparently good alternatives to or modifications of previous ideas, or with his own plans and lies, fooling me and then leading me to his own conclusions. This is why discernment, especially in important matters, can take time. I need to see where the thoughts proceed to, how I feel after a while, in order to evaluate not just the beginning (which can be from the Lord, and is when the consolation comes without adequate cause) but the middle and the end. Discernment, too, often needs discernment. In discernment, and especially in discerning a discernment itself, sometimes a prayerful friend, a regular confessor, or a spiritual director can be helpful.

*

Prayer.

Lord Jesus, teach me the discernment of spirits. Give me the gift of being able to distinguish the impulses and urgings of your Spirit from any impulses and urgings that come from the world, the flesh, or the devil. Give me the grace, Lord, to weigh ideas and proposals and plans with you in order to determine if they are truly from you.

I do not ask you, Lord, for the wisdom that the world gives, but for your gift of discernment, for the wisdom you give that lovingly sees the source of thoughts and feelings. Give me the discerning wisdom that judges according to your Holy Spirit. *Amen.*

9

DISCERNMENT OF SPIRITS: DECIDING

Ignatius of Loyola applies his rules for the discernment of spirits to decision-making. I want to make my decisions in accord with the ideas and inner urgings that come from the good spirit, and not in accord with ideas or urgings that come from the evil spirit. I want to find out what God's will is for me in a particular case or instance. What is the Lord calling me to do? Among the options open to me, which one is from the Lord? Discernment of spirits can be the foundation for the discernment of what the Lord calls me to here and now, in these particular circumstances. How can I make decisions, especially important decisions, on the basis of discerning spirits? How can I know what God's will is for me in a particular case?

Making Decisions

Let us say that I want to discern God's will for me in an important matter. I have already gathered the pertinent facts, the relevant information. Perhaps, as needed, I have consulted one or two other persons. At any rate, I now have an adequate grasp of the problem. But I remain unable to come to a decision; I still do not know what the Lord wants me to do in this particular matter. I have already prayed for the Lord's light and guidance in marshalling the data, in consulting persons or books or documents, in going over pros and cons. Now, I take my decision-to-be-made explicitly to the Lord to see what he wants me to do.

Jesus is the Lord of my life, and I want to bring my decision to him, to make my decision under his lordship. In a brief period of contemplation, of looking with faith and love at the Lord, I try to think through the matter with him — not in a logical and highly reasoned way, but mulling things over with the Lord, in the prayer zone of his love for me. With Jesus, looking him in the eye as it were, contemplating him, I ponder my possible alternative decisions, my options in the case under consideration. I lift up to Jesus, in turn, the various possible ways I could decide. *I see how I feel about each one in terms of my relationship with the Lord.*

In this way, I exercise the discernment of spirits regarding each one of the options open to me. This discernment process has as its purpose to find out which of the options or possible decisions is inspired by the Lord, has his Spirit at its origin, is what he wants me to do. Ordinarily, over a period of time relative to the importance of the decision in question, I will come to a conclusion. I lift up to the Lord all the options, discerning as to the source (good spirit or not) of each one, for a few minutes once or twice every day. I do this in an explicit way, taking Jesus' loving care for me seriously, trying truly to find out what he wants, consulting him with seriousness and with trust.

After a certain amount of this, or perhaps right at the beginning and from then on, I will feel consolation with regard to one of the options. When I "look the Lord in the eye" about one possible decision, I will consistently feel a kind of fitting-ness, a rightness, that this is right. Or a consistent peace and interior harmony. Or possibly a real joy and gladness of heart. This is a sign that the particular option is from the good spirit.

The Key to Decision-Making

The key, then, is this: how right, how comfortable in the Lord's presence, do I feel in terms of each of the options? But how can I be sure? I will probably not attain complete certainty. I can stay with my conclusion (that this particular possible decision is the one I should make) for some days, testing it, holding it up for confirmation to the Lord to see if it is really from him. If it is, the consolation will continue. I can continue for a while to discern my discernment. And then I make and carry out my decision.

I can trust the Lord, and I can trust his Holy Spirit in my heart. The Holy Spirit will give me a knowledge through love of the nature of my interior experience. He will show me which of the ideas in my head, in my heart, is due to his inspiration. I may need some time, several days maybe, to sift things out, to distinguish my own natural likes and dislikes, tastes, fears, prejudices, feelings, from the movements of the good and bad spirits. And, even at the end, I cannot be absolutely sure that my decision is right.

Or can I? In a sense, yes. What the Lord wants me to do is what I think he wants me to do. So, if I do what I think, even without complete certainty of what his will for me is, then I am certainly doing his will for me.

If my decision involves another person, I may need to pray with that person; a husband and wife may need to come to a joint decision. In that case, they will need to discern each individually, to pool the results of their prayerful discernment, and to pray together. Some decisions are group decisions and call for a discernment on the part of each member of the group.

The process of communal discernment, where two or more persons have to make the decision together, might go like this. Each one prays alone, discerning. They come together — not to discuss, but to pool, to listen to the prayerful conclusion reached by each one. Then they pray together. If unanimity is not reached, then the process can be repeated until it is, or until a vote of some kind is taken.

The Basis of Discernment and Decisions

The Lord calls me to discern what, in my own interior experience, comes from the good spirit and what does not. And he calls me to make my decisions, especially the important ones, in consultation with him, on the basis of a discernment of spirits. However, for the discernment of spirits, one particular condition in my life needs to be fulfilled: I need to be a person of prayer, and —going further — a person of contemplative prayer.

The discernment of spirits has a strongly contemplative dimension. The foundational relationship in the process of the discernment of spirits is a personal and contemplative relationship with the Lord. If I do not have a regular prayer life, and even regular contemplation in my life, I will not have the necessary relationship with the Lord for the discernment of spirits and for discernment-based decision-making.

To put it another way, to exercise the discernment of spirits, I need not only contemplative prayer regularly, on a daily basis, but also to fulfill in my life the conditions of contemplation: time in contemplation, freedom of heart, childlike simplicity in my relationship with the Lord (see Chapter 1). Unless I devote time regularly and faithfully in contemplating the Lord, I will hardly be able to have the kind of "face-to-face" relationship I need with him in order to discern what is from the good spirit and what is not. Unless my heart is free, I will be so bound by my own inordinate attachments that I will not be able to exercise discernment. My possessiveness will tie me to certain options that gratify my own selfishness; I may tell myself that those options are from the good spirit, but I will not experience the inimitable peace and consoling rightness about those choices, I will not experience the consolation that comes from the good spirit. And unless I have a childlike simplicity in my relationship with the Lord, how can I look at him with the eyes of faith and trust and love, quietly and simply, to find out which of the ideas I have are truly ideas of his?

If I do have the habit of contemplative prayer in my life, then I will find not only that I can effectively evaluate my interior experience and arrive at right decisions through the exercise of the discernment of spirits, but also that the discernment of spirits can, so to speak, broaden out and penetrate my whole life. If I habitually discern the spirits at work in my heart and act on what I discern as coming from the good spirit, then, over a period of time, I will learn to follow the lead of the good spirit in whatever I choose, in whatever I do. I will learn to choose and to act according to the way the Holy Spirit leads me. I will be "walking in the Spirit." I will live contemplatively, my eyes always on the Lord, walking always in his Spirit. My whole life will be a decision for Jesus.

Walking in the Spirit

Saint Paul tells us, "If we live in the Spirit, then also let us walk in the Spirit" (Galatians 5:25; see 5:16). To live in the Spirit means to have God's new life in me, to *be* in a new way — a new creation. To walk in the Spirit means to *act* in a certain way, to take a direction and move that way. To walk in the Spirit means to live out, in my daily behavior, the discernment of spirits.

When I live according to the Holy Spirit, I am free. I can make my choices not because laws and rules bind me and determine my conduct. I am free from the bondage of the law (Romans 8:3), and I am free to do what the law says not because the law coerces me but because the Spirit empowers me to know and choose and do what the Lord wants. My choices are not just "head choices" based on knowledge of what is right, but "heart choices" based on knowledge through love of what the Lord calls me to.

I act according to the interior law of the Spirit (Romans 8:2), setting my mind "not on the things of the flesh," but "on the things of the Spirit; . . . to set the mind on the Spirit is life and peace" (Romans 8:5-6). The Spirit himself helps me to pray; "the Spirit helps us in our weakness, for we do not know how to pray as we should, but the Spirit himself intercedes for us with sighs that words cannot express" (Romans 8:26). With the Spirit praying in me, I can ask the Lord to guide my choices, to help me in my decisions, and I can be "led by the Spirit of God" (Romans 8:14).

Because I have been renewed by the Holy Spirit, "born anew" (1 Peter 1:3 and 23), because I am a new creation "in Christ Jesus" (Ephesians 2:10), because I now through the Spirit share in a mysterious way in the very life of God, I am "tuned in" to the Lord and to what he wants. My life is lined up in view of God and what his will is for me, so that I can spontaneously know or feel which choices are the right ones. And I know when the Spirit is guiding me, when I am choosing and deciding in the Spirit, because I experience the consolation of the fruits of the Spirit: "love, joy, peace, patience, kindness, goodness, faithfulness, gentleness, self-control" (Galatians 5:22).

*

Prayer.

Lord Jesus, teach me your ways. Teach me to walk always in your Holy Spirit. With the help of your grace, I ask that all my choices be in accord with my basic choice of you as my

Savior. I ask that all my decisions, the daily quickly-made decisions and the important decisions of my life, be made in accord with your Spirit, in accord with the total plan you have for me in your heart.

Teach me to make my important decisions in consultation with you, discerning what is from you and what is not. And teach me to choose rightly, in harmony with your Spirit in my heart, when I make all my small daily decisions.

Teach me to walk in your Spirit and to experience the consolation of the fruits of the Spirit, of the love you pour into my heart through your Spirit, of the joy and peace that you give, of the patience and goodness and kindness that your Spirit empowers me to have, and of the gentleness and the self-control that flow from a basic trust in your guidance.

Teach me to walk in your Spirit. *Amen*.

10

DISCERNMENT OF SPIRITS:
SPIRITUAL COMBAT

The metaphor that Ignatius of Loyola, in the *Spiritual Exercises*, finds most suitable for describing Christian life is that of warfare. This vision of Christian life as warfare, with Jesus Christ and against the powers of darkness, runs through Ignatius' "Rules for the Discernment of Spirits" and is dramatically expressed in his "Meditation on the Two Standards" (*Spiritual Exercises*), sections 136-148). The "Meditation on the Two Standards" asks the person making the meditation to imagine Satan and Jesus as the commanders of two opposed armies, each with its own flag, its own strategy and tactics and program for victory. The person making the exercises concludes the "Meditation" by formally asking to be accepted under the standard (the flag) of Jesus and to imitate him in all things (section 147).

The metaphor of warfare enables Ignatius to stress many things he finds important in Christian living: loyalty to the Lord, generosity in making sacrifices, selfless service, courage and faithfulness in times of darkness and difficulty. And, also, it can lead to a realistic appreciation of the existence and tricks of the devil.

When talk turns, as it does once in a great while, to the devil or to matters diabolical, I can find myself touched by the innocence of those persons who no longer give credence to the devil's existence, who hold him and all evil spirits to be holdovers from medieval times, mere popular symbols of evil in the world. People who have had so little experience of evil do edify me; they have surely met sin and evil, but not to the extent of recognizing a personal evil force at the heart of the mystery of iniquity.

On the other hand, the naïveté of persons who ignore the action of the devil can be dangerous. They go to battle unarmed and not knowing even of the existence of the enemy. They can get hurt, and those around them whom they should protect can get hurt too. "We are not contending against flesh and blood, but against the principalities, against the powers, against the world rulers of this present darkness, against the spiritual hosts of wickedness" (Ephesians 6:11). So let us, following Paul's advice, "put on the whole armor of God" that we "may be able to stand against the wiles of the devil" (Ephesians 6:10).

This armor consists of faith, hope, love, truth and right-eousness, the gospel of peace, and the word of God. It consists also of the commonsense pastoral practice of Christian tradition. An important element of that tradition, one we have almost lost sight of, is "rebuking the devil". All of us should be familiar with it so that we can more effectively fight against the presence of evil in our lives.

Evil Spirits Exist

Theology has neglected the significance — the meaning for us today — of the exorcisms in the New Testament. Because the Holy Spirit is with Jesus in power, Jesus casts out evil spirits, and his many exorcisms herald the presence of the kingdom of God. "But if it is through the Spirit of God that I cast devils out, then know that the kingdom of God has overtaken you" (Matthew 12:28). Moreover, Jesus teaches his disciples to exorcise demons.

If theology has neglected the existence of Satan, of evil spirits, of personalized forces of evil in the world, even in the face of overwhelming biblical data, Church teaching, on the other hand, has regularly referred to the existence of the devil and of devils. In 1972, Pope Paul VI spoke clearly: "Evil is not merely a lack of something, but an effective agent, a living spiritual being, perverted and perverting. A terrible reality. Mysterious and frightening. . . . We know that this dark and and misfortunes in human history. . . . It is not a question of trecherous cunning; he is the secret enemy that sows errors and misfortunes in human history. . . . It is not a question of one Devil but of many. . . . This question of the Devil and the influence he can exert on individual persons as well as on communities, whole societies, and events, is a very important chapter of Catholic doctrine" (*L'Osservatore Romano*, English language edition, Nov. 23, 1972, p. 3).

Evil spirits, then, have an important if obscure role in the world. The "prince of this world" exercises what power he has chiefly through his action on individual persons. He is the tempter, the seducer, the evil counsellor, the promoter of evil projects; he deceives, he blinds, he corrupts. He is "the father" of liars and assassins and of those who do not love their brothers and sisters.

With regard to diabolical influence on individual persons, theologians distinguish between possession, oppression, and temptation. The signs of possible possession are given by the *Roman Ritual* (ed. P. Weller, Milwaukee: Bruce, 1964, p. 641) in the section on exorcisms; they are the ability to speak or understand a previously unlearned language, to see future or distant things, extraordinarily great strength — especially when these signs are found together. Cases of possession seem extremely rare. Father de Tonquédec, S.J., official exorcist for the Paris archdiocese, said after twenty years of practice that he had never met even one.

Oppression occurs when a demon or demons exercise some control over a person, torment him, sometimes provide him with extraordinary powers, but do not deprive him entirely or almost entirely of free choice. Grave and rare cases of oppression can seem almost like possession. Less serious oppression, common enough, can account for the apparently compulsive element in some cases of habitual sin such as hatred or anger or resentment, or gluttony or lust. Oppression is sometimes a partial explanation, certainly not always or most often, of habitual fear, sadness, irrational guilt feelings, anguish, scrupulosity. When temptations are sudden, strong, persistent, and hard to account for by natural means, we can conclude that there is a special intervention on the part of the devil; in such cases, we call this intervention "oppression."

Temptations can come from the world, the flesh, or the devil. Temptations that derive wholly or partly from the action of evil spirits can come and go in a transitory way, or they can persist in an aggravating and continuous manner in a way that can hardly be distinguished from oppression. Often, one can identify or at least guess at the diabolical origin (total or partial) of a temptation by a certain manifest compulsion coupled with a certain strangeness or irrationality or even weirdness.

But, after all, has not the modern science of psychology and psychiatry shown us the psychological origins of much behavior that used to be considered diabolical in origin? Even granted the existence of the devil, and if we grant that he can influence human behavior, how do you know what comes from mental illness or neurotic tendencies and what comes from demonic influence? Do we not risk diagnosing mental illness as diabolical oppression, and so do more harm than good?

Mental illness and the influence of evil spirits are two different things, and we want to avoid reducing all diabolical influence to mental illness, or reducing mental illness to the work of the devil. And, in practice, it is difficult and sometimes impossible to know the exact origins of problems; mental illness and diabolical influence can be inextricably tangled. The pastoral response is, of course, to try whatever seems appropriate under the circumstances, and to follow up whatever approach seems to be working. This applies to psychological therapy, to psychiatric treatment, and to taking authority over evil spirits.

Authority over Evil Spirits

The fact that the devil and his minions exist should be seen in the light of the victory of Jesus' resurrection. Christ's triumph over evil, not only during his public ministry but especially in his resurrection, helps us to avoid any kind of Manichean dualism regarding God and the devil. God wins. The devil has been beaten. As Christians, we share in Christ's victory over the powers of darkness, and because we are his, members of his body, sharing through grace in his victory, we have authority over evil spirits.

Jesus has given us this authority to use. And this authority over the devil and over all evil spirits, the authority that Jesus has given to his Church and to every Christian, holds its power from him who has given it. So it is not necessary to embellish the authority of Jesus — which he gives to us — with shouting or with efforts to converse in some way with evil spirits. This authority is powerful enough to stand on its own, to be used calmly and quietly and briefly.

In the Protestant Pentecostal tradition, Christian authority over evil spirits is sometimes used dramatically and even in a way that seems theatrical. Some of this style can still be found here and there in neo-pentecostalism and in the Catholic charismatic renewal. In pagan religions, particularly in animist religions, the drama takes on great theatricality. I have witnessed an attempted exorcism by a Ugandan witch doctor, complete with chants, shouts, and the beating of drums; the idea, I believe, was to frighten the evil spirits away. The Catholic tradition, on the other hand, has always observed a certain moderation of style which derives not from some sense of good taste but from faith, buttressed by experience, in the power of the name of Jesus. There is no need to embellish the authority Jesus gives us, we should use it firmly and with faith in him.

Rebuking the Devil

The most common way that evil spirits attack human beings is by temptation. Not all temptations, obviously, come from the devil, but some do. In getting rid of temptations that seem to or that might at least partly come from the devil, we can use the advice of Ignatius Loyola in his "Rules for the Discernment of Spirits" in his manual of *Spiritual Exercises*.

Throughout the *Exercises*, Ignatius refers to the devil as "the enemy of human nature." He clearly had no illusions about the devil and his minions, and we know that his "rules" for dealing with evil spirits find their basis in Ignatius' own experience as well as in the Church's pastoral tradition. That he did perform exorcisms is commemorated in an old painting hanging in the hall just outside his rooms in the Jesuit theologate in Rome; it shows Ignatius exorcising a person from whose mouth issue three or four tiny black stick figures, going up into the air. The ingenuous quality of the painting contrasts with Ignatius' own hardheaded realism in dealing with the devil.

The "enemy of human nature," Ignatius teaches in his

"Rules for the Discernment of Spirits," acts like a military chief; "he prowls around and explores on all sides all our virtues, theological, cardinal, and moral, and where he finds us weakest, . . . there he makes his attack, and strives to take us by storm" (*Spiritual Exercises*, section 327). We might expect to be tempted at our weak points.

Again, writes Ignatius, the devil "acts like a false lover, inasmuch as he wishes to remain hidden and undiscovered; for as this false man . . . paying court to the daughter of some honest father or the wife of some honest man, wishes his conversations and insinuations to be kept secret," so the devil "is very displeased when they [his wiles and deceits] are discovered to a good confessor or some other spiritual person who knows his frauds and malice" (*Spiritual Exercises*, section 326).

Most importantly for our purpose here, Ignatius describes the devil as acting "like a woman, inasmuch as he is weak in spite of himself, but strong in will." Just as a woman backs down when quarrelling with a man if the man is uncompromising, but acts most firmly if the man behaves in a weak way, so too the devil runs when we face him fearlessly and becomes ferocious if we act fearfully (*Spiritual Exercises*, section 325). Whatever one thinks of Ignatius' evaluation of a quarrelling woman, he did understand the devil, and his advice is practical.

The traditional Christian practice of "rebuking the devil" holds today as valid and as useful as ever. One prays briefly, asking the Lord or his mother for help, and one simply addresses a command to whatever evil spirit or spirits might be present. For example, "Leave me immediately in Jesus' name." Or: "Spirit of fear, leave me immediately in Jesus' name." Or:

"Spirit of anger (or of lust, or whatever), go now in Jesus' name and never come back."

The Lord has given Christians authority over evil spirits. It works. We should take that authority and use it to defend ourselves against temptations that come from the devil. Let me give one example. A man once asked my advice; he had been falling into serious sins of a perverted sexual nature, and felt very weak as well as ashamed of himself. He asked how he could avoid these sins. The element of compulsion as well as a certain strangeness about the sins, together with the fact that the man had lost so much self-esteem and hated himself (always a goal of the devil), led me to suggest that perhaps he was tempted by the devil. I suggested that the next time he felt tempted he should assume authority and command the devil to leave him in Jesus' name. He did, and he had no more trouble from that time on.

Any time I sense the presence of evil spirits or have reason to suspect their influence, either an influence of temptation or of oppression, whether on me or on someone else or in a particular group or a particular place, I can use the authority Jesus gives me. I can pray to Jesus briefly for help. I can then command the evil spirits to be gone: "Evil spirits, leave immediately in Jesus' name." And then I can pray for a new outpouring of the Holy Spirit for myself or for the person or persons I felt were being influenced (tempted or oppressed).

There is certainly nothing to be afraid of. On the contrary, evil spirits are afraid of you. You *have* the victory over them in Jesus. He wins. And so, in him, do you.

*

Prayer.

Lord Jesus, thank you for the power of the authority to command and to send away the devil and all the bad spirits that work for him. Thank you, Jesus, for entrusting me with this power. Teach me to use it well and without fear.

Thank you for calling me to your side, for putting me under your flag, in the spiritual warfare of this world. Thank you for arming me with the whole battle equipment of God, with the truth buckled around my waist, "with the breastplate of righteousness and the boots of the spreading of the gospel of peace, with the shield of faith and the helmet of salvation and the sword of the Spirit, which is the word of God" (Ephesians 6:14-17).

I go forward, Lord, without fear, trusting in you and protected by the merits of your precious blood shed for me. *Amen.*

11

LOVE AND DISCERNMENT

Love is the hallmark of Christianity. Love is more important than knowledge, and the highest knowledge is contemplative — knowledge through love. The most important love is not the love I have for God, but God's love for me. The love of God manifested — made incarnate for me — comes in and through the heart of Jesus.

Jesus' Love

I can ask the question: in what way does Jesus Christ love us, love each one of us, love me personally? And I can find elements of an answer to my question in the teaching of Jesus himself. He teaches us to love our enemies and to do good even to those who hate us, to bless those who curse us and to pray for those who abuse us, to offer the other cheek to whoever strikes me, not to withhold my shirt from the man who steals my coat, to give to those who beg from me, and to act toward others as we would like them to act toward us (Luke 6:27-31). If Jesus teaches this kind of radical, far-reaching, even extreme way of loving, then I can be sure that this is, also, the way that he loves me.

"If you love those who love you, what credit is that to you? For even sinners love those who love them. And if you do good to those who do good to you, what credit is that to you? For even sinners do the same. And if you lend to those from whom you hope to receive, what credit is that to you? Even sinners lend to sinners, to receive as much again. But love your enemies, and do good, and lend, expecting nothing in return" (Luke 6:32-35). These words of Jesus tell me how he loves and, in particular, how he loves me: completely and generously even when I do not love him, when I am myself selfish and sinful. Jesus, as the Son and the Revelation of the Father, shows forth himself the qualities of the Father's love: "He is kind to the ungrateful and the selfish" (Luke 6:35). Jesus is merciful in love, just as the Father is (see Luke 6:36).

"Judge not, and you will not be judged," Jesus teaches (Luke 6:37). So I can clearly expect him not to judge me; if he teaches me not to judge others, then I can be sure he does not judge me. "Do not condemn others, and you will not be condemned" (Luke 6:37). I know, then, that Jesus in his love for me does not condemn me no matter what my behavior has been, no matter what bad attitudes I have had. "Forgive and you will be forgiven; give and it will be given to you" (Luke 6:37-38). Jesus teaches generous forgiveness and, more generally, generosity in everything; he teaches me to forgive and to give, to be a forgiver and a giver. I can be certain, therefore, that he forgives me.

But what, I might ask, is love? What precisely does it mean; how can we describe love? Saint Paul gives us the answer. He writes: "Love is patient and kind. Love is never jealous. It is not boastful. Love is not puffed up with pride. It is not bad-mannered. Love does not insist on having its own way. Love does not take offence. It does not hold grudges. Love takes no pleasure in what is wrong; it rejoices in what is right and true. Love stands ready always to excuse, to trust, to hope, and to bear all things" (1 Cor. 13:4-7). I can take Paul's descriptive definition of love and use it to better understand Jesus' love for me. What is the quality of Jesus' love for me? How does he love me?

I know from John's gospel that God is love. And I know that Jesus is God. It is correct and good theology, then, to say that — if Jesus is God, and God is love — then Jesus is love. If Jesus is love, I can substitute the word "Jesus" for the word "love" in Paul's passage about love. What will this give me? A description of Jesus-as-loving-me. It will give me a personality profile of Jesus.

How does Jesus love me? Jesus is patient and kind. Jesus is never jealous. He is not boastful. Jesus is not puffed up with pride. He is not bad-mannered. Jesus does not insist on having his own way. Jesus does not take offence. He does not hold grudges. Jesus takes no pleasure in what is wrong; he rejoices in what is right and true. Jesus stands ready always to excuse, to trust, to hope, and to bear all things.

This is the quality of Jesus' love for me. This is how he loves me. What is more, in his love for me, he sends me his Holy Spirit, who is Love.

The Holy Spirit

The Father's love is made incarnate for us and manifested to us in Jesus Christ. And the love of the Father and of Jesus is poured into our hearts through their Holy Spirit (Romans 5:5).

The Holy Spirit is the mutual love between Jesus and the Father. Jesus loves the Father. And the Father loves Jesus. The love between them is a Person who is Love. That Person is the Holy Spirit, God, the Spirit of God.

Jesus and the Father send me their Holy Spirit. When the Spirit dwells in my heart, he catches me up in Jesus' love for the Father and in the Father's love for Jesus. He takes me right into the interior life of God, into the community life of love of the Three Divine Persons. I am caught up into the Trinity.

The Holy Spirit relates me to Jesus and the Father; because he is their mutual love, he relates me to them in love. I can go to the Father without fear, in love, because his Spirit lives in me. I can come to Jesus in trust and in love because the Spirit of Jesus dwells in my heart.

Discernment through Love

The discernment of spirits is always in and through the love that is poured into my heart through the Holy Spirit. The gift of love, the gift that the Father and Jesus give me in my heart through their Spirit, empowers me to love, raises up and enriches my capacity to love.

This gift of love enables me to enter into contemplation, to look with the eyes of faith at the Lord, to keep my eyes fixed on Jesus — because contemplation is knowledge through love.

Discernment, the discernment of spirits, is judgment based on knowledge through love; it is judgment in the context of contemplation. Discernment is contemplative judgment, contemplative evaluation. And it is always made in and through love.

We can learn about love and about discernment from a brief look at the First Letter to the Corinthians. They had a lot of problems, and those problems were the reason for Paul's letter to them. Their biggest problem was that they lacked love, lacking love they lacked discernment, and lacking discernment they made several bad evaluations and judgments and fell into quite serious difficulties. The Corinthians did not seem to know that Christian knowledge is knowledge through love. They had a wrong idea of Christian knowledge, and they unfortunately acted on that idea with disastrous results. The letter constitutes Paul's effort to straighten out their thinking.

Judging from Paul's first letter to them, the Christians at Corinth put high value on certain gifts of the Spirit, especially gifts of knowledge, wisdom, and any gift, such as prophesying in an incomprehensible language, that appeared to manifest mysterious and arcane knowledge. In letters to other churches Paul praises those to whom he writes for their faith, hope, love; but he thanks God that those in Corinth are "enriched in him with all speech and all knowledge" (1 Cor 1:5). Paul praises them not for any virtue, but for charisms. The omission of faith, hope, and love indicates problems; and Paul will speak of these problems in the course of the letter.

What is more, after thanking God for their gifts of speech and knowledge, Paul gives them a teaching that indicates that they lack Christian wisdom. He contrasts the wisdom of speech with the word of the cross (1:17-18; see 2:2). Paul did not come preaching with enticing words, but in the Spirit and in power (2:4). Later on, he will point out that if anyone should have all knowledge but lacks love, he is nothing (13:2).

God has made foolish the wisdom of the world (1:20); God's foolishness is wiser than men (1:25); God has chosen what is foolish in the world to shame the wise.

It becomes clear as the letter progresses that the Corinthians, in fact, do lack wisdom; they lack good judgment and Christian discernment. So Paul cannot address them as spiritual men, but as men of the flesh (3:1). There is among them jealousy and strife. They lack unity, and the church is breaking down into factions, some for Paul, some for Apollos, some for Cephas (1:11-16; 3:3-23). They seem divided even over issues like whether or not women should wear veils in the assembly (11:2-16). And they bring law suits against one another in the civil courts (6:1-7). They wrong and defraud one another (6:7).

The Corinthians lack not only wisdom but basic prudence and commonsense. At their celebration of the Lord's supper, "each goes ahead with his own meal, and one is hungry and another drunk" (11:21). They seem to have serious problems with sexual morality (6:13-20), and tolerate even incest (5:1-13). Some, it seems, frequent prostitutes (6:15).

The prayer assemblies apparently are chaotic, with many

prophecies in tongues and few or no interpretations, even several persons at a time prophesying in tongues (chapter 14). Anyone who has ever heard a prophecy in tongues at a pentecostal or charismatic prayer meeting can imagine the disorder in the Corinthians' meetings.

Furthermore, their gifts of speech and knowledge have made them arrogant, inflated their pride, made them puffed up (4:6: see 4:18; 5:2; 13:5). In the light of all this, one might read Paul's description of love in chapter thirteen, verses 4 to 7, as a kind of list of the Corinthians' fundamental defects: to be unkind, impatient, puffed up, selfish, bad-mannered, irritable, grudge-holding, lacking faith, lacking hope, and, of course, lacking love.

The heart of the First Letter to the Corinthians is the thirteenth chapter. What the Corinthian Christians need and lack most is love. And Paul encourages them to pray for the charisms, but above all to pray for love. Love is more than a charism. It is a way, a way of life, a road, a life-pathway (12:31). And without love, the charisms are nothing. Clearly, Paul wants the Christians at Corinth to foster and use the gifts of knowledge and wisdom for which he praised them early in the letter. Knowledge not informed by love is nothing; wisdom without Christian love is only worldly wisdom; every gift must be used in love, informed by love.

Lacking true knowledge, they fail to exercise Christian discernment, which is knowledge through love. And lacking discernment, they choose wrongly and fall into all the problems that Paul points at in the letter.

Listening to Jesus

"To know Jesus" means more than having knowledge about him. It means to experience interpersonal contact with him. It means to know him through love. "To listen to his voice" means to distinguish Jesus' voice from all the noise and static that goes on in and around me; it means discernment.

John's gospel gives us these words of Jesus: "I know my own, and mine know me, just as the Father knows me and I know the Father" (John 10:14-15). How does Jesus know me and I know him? In the same way as the Father knows Jesus and Jesus knows the Father. Jesus and the Father know one another in and through the Holy Spirit, who is Love and who binds them together in one Divine Nature. So too, Jesus and I know one another in and through the Holy Spirit, who is Love and who binds us together.

Jesus continues along the same lines: "My sheep listen to my voice, and I know them, and they follow me. I give them everlasting life. They will never be lost, and no one will ever take them out of my hands. My Father who has given them to me is greater than all, and no one can take them out of the Father's hands. The Father and I are one" (John 10:27-30).

Jesus holds me in his hands. I belong to him. He knows me and he leads me to greater knowledge and love himself. He gives me the gift of listening to his voice, the gift of discernment, of evaluating and judging-through-love. And I can rest secure in his hands because I am in the Father's hands, the Father has given me to Jesus.

*

Prayer.

Lord Jesus, give me the gift of love.

Teach me to walk always in the path of love that you pour into my heart through the gift of your Holy Spirit.

Teach me to know you better and better through the love that you pour into my heart through your Spirit. Teach me to pray contemplatively. And guide me every day so that I walk always with my eyes on you. Let me walk always in your Spirit.

Teach me, Jesus, discernment. Give me and increase in me the gift of listening to your voice, of knowing what is your voice. Make me sensitive and docile to the urgings that come from your Spirit. Let me walk always in your Spirit. *Amen.*

12

DISCERNMENT AND THE
MOTHER OF JESUS

The New Testament presents us with a model for the discernment of spirits in the person and the life of Mary, the mother of Jesus. Mary, partly as a result of her first recorded discernment at the announcement by the angel that she was to be the mother of Jesus, became a channel for God's saving grace for the world.

Model of Discernment

Mary, at the words of the angel Gabriel, "Hail, favored one, the Lord is with you," was "greatly disturbed, and considered what kind of greeting this could be" (Luke 1:28-29). Her perplexity increased at the message that she would have a child. The result of her on-the-spot discernment was, "Behold the handmaid of the Lord; may it happen to me according to your word" (Luke 1:38). On Mary's discernment depended her assent; before saying "yes" to God, she needed to discern whether what was happening really was of God or not. Having discerned its divine origin, she gave her unconditional "yes" to the will of God.

Mary continued to exercise discernment. We know that she not only kept in her heart all the things that happened, the birth of Jesus and the visit of the shepherds, but that she "pondered" them "in her heart," looking for their meaning with the light that God gave her. At the wedding feast of Cana, Mary knew with a kind of instinctive discernment that Jesus would somehow do what she asked him — solve the problem of the wine lack at the feast. "They have no wine," Mary said with confidence to Jesus, simply presenting the problem to him. Then, to the waiters, she said, "Whatever he tells you, do it" (John 2:3-5); she knew by discernment that he would remedy the situation.

Mary's discernment extended even to the acceptance of the fact of Jesus' death on the cross. Mary at the foot of the cross lived out in action her initial "yes" to God at the announcement of the angel Gabriel. Her discernment led her, in terrible grief and suffering, to the acceptance of the crucifixion as God's will and plan.

The presence in the upper room of Mary, praying with the disciples and waiting to be "clothed with power from on high" (Luke 24:49) indicates that there was and is more to Mary's role in God's plan for our salvation than to be simply a model. We need to go back to the annunciation, to Mary's assent to

God's plan, to see further her significance regarding discernment in our lives, regarding the Lord's call to us to "walk always in the Spirit" (Galatians 5:25).

Mother of Discernment

The basic New Testament fact about Mary is that she is Jesus' mother. Her acceptance of the angel's word, "be it done unto me" which was at the same time her acceptance of God's plan for her motherhood of Jesus, determined her place in the overall economy of salvation. Mary became Jesus' mother. The point is that Mary is Jesus' mother *now*; we do not say that she was his mother, but that she is the mother of Jesus. Her relationship of maternity persists. Her motherhood is a relationship based on past historical fact (she conceived, bore, gave birth to, nurtured Jesus), but it remains as a permanent relationship. One's mother is always one's mother.

Mary, as Jesus' mother, is in some way the point of contact between Jesus and the world, including all of us. The Word of God took on humanity in and through Mary, became human by having a human mother. Jesus became our Savior and Mediator with the Father, our only Savior and Mediator, through Mary. I am related to Jesus as to my Savior, and to the Father through and in Jesus. Because Jesus came to us first through Mary, and because that fact established a permanent relationship, he still comes to us through Mary.

What does that mean? What does it mean objectively, in the nature of things? And what does it mean for me? Objectively, I am related to Jesus through Mary. Christians, then, are in some way children of Mary because through her they are related to Jesus and incorporated into the body of her Son which is the Church. It would be quite incorrect to say that I am related to Mary through Jesus. That would put Mary above Jesus, or at least equal to him, on the same level. And that would detract from Jesus' uniqueness as our only Mediator with the Father. No, we are related to Jesus through Mary because he comes to us now through her, just as he did at his incarnation. Mary is my mother in the order of grace.

"This maternity of Mary in the order of grace," declares the Second Vatican Council's document on the Church (*Lumen gentium*), "began with the consent which she gave in faith at the Annunciation and which she sustained, without wavering, beneath the cross; this maternity will last without interruption; . . . taken up into heaven, by her intercession . . . she continues to win for us gifts of eternal salvation" (article 62). Mary prays for me, intercedes for me, like a mother. Her intercession, as at Cana, helps me in concrete everyday situations.

Because Mary is the mother of grace in my life, she can be considered the mother of the grace of discernment. She helps me, by her intercession with Jesus, to listen always to his voice, to discern what is from him, and to say always "yes" to what he calls me to.

What does this mean for me subjectively? What does it mean for my life in Jesus, in his Spirit? The fact that Mary is my mother in the order of grace does not at all mean that I *must* pray to her or ask her intercession. I can go straight to Jesus. But it does mean that I *can* go to Jesus explicitly through Mary, that I can get Mary to ask Jesus for me, or I can go to Jesus with her.

Mary is my mother, and I can learn discernment from her. From Mary I can learn to walk in the Spirit.

*

Prayer.

Mary, I ask you to pray for me for the gift of discernment. Intercede for me with Jesus; ask him to give me, and in great abundance, the gift of listening to his voice, of walking in his Spirit, of following him in love. Take me with you to Jesus now.

Jesus, I come to you with your mother, Mary. I ask you for the gift of discernment. You are one in the Holy Spirit with the Father. Make me more one with you in the Holy Spirit. You always listen to the Father; teach me to listen to you. You always do what the Father asks; help me to respond generously to you, saying always "yes" to you. *Amen.*

A FINAL NOTE

The gifts of contemplation and discernment are not given in isolation nor are they for us alone. They are gifts of prayer. Gifts of prayer come to us in community, and form us and mould us so that the Lord can use us for others, to build up the communities we are part of, and to speak his word to others.

"And when they had prayed, the place in which they were assembled was shaken, and they were all filled with the Holy Spirit and spoke the word of God with boldness. The multitude of them that believed were one heart and soul, and no one said that what he had was his own; everything was in common. And with great power the apostles gave witness to the resurrection of the Lord Jesus, and great grace was upon them all. No one among them was needy, ... because distribution was made to each one according to his need" (Acts 4:31-35). Prayer fills me with the Spirit of Jesus. And the Spirit anoints me to share with others. To share Jesus by proclaiming him and witnessing to him in appropriate ways, not timidly but with courage, boldly. And to share with others my possessions, to go out in love to my brothers and sisters in need, to share my gifts and my trust in the Lord and even my material possessions.

The purpose of this book is to help you to pray. More broadly, it was written to help you to "live in the Spirit" and to "walk in the Spirit," with Jesus, together with all who listen to his voice.

May the Lord help you to grow in union with him in contemplation and in discernment. May he teach you to live and walk in his Spirit. And may he lead you to love and serve and minister to him in your brothers and sisters.